LITERARY
NEW HAMPSHIRE
A History & Guide

GARY CROOKER

Foreword by Joe Adamowicz

THE
History
PRESS

Published by The History Press
Charleston, SC
www.historypress.com

First published 2023

Manufactured in the United States

ISBN 9781467153782

Library of Congress Control Number: 2023932160

Notice: The information in this book is true and complete to the best of our knowledge. It is offered without guarantee on the part of the author or The History Press. The author and The History Press disclaim all liability in connection with the use of this book.

CONTENTS

CONTENTS

ACKNOWLEDGEMENTS

There are so many folks who have been helpful to me on this project that my only worry is forgetting someone. If I have, I apologize in advance.

Assistance with matters technical I could not have done without. For that, I thank editor Mike Kinsella at The History Press. Also invaluable with that aid have been Elizabeth Crooker and Melissa Crooker. Thanks for your help and, most importantly, your patience.

Masheri Chapelle at the New Hampshire Writer's Project, Mary Russell at the New Hampshire Center for the Book, the Exeter LitFest, Simon Parsons at the Fells and Andrew Cushing with the NH Preservation Alliance all were helpful and prompt with any inquiries I had. Stasia Millet of the Harriet Wilson Project also has my thanks for her help. The same goes for Robert Perreault, author of *Franco-American Life and Culture in Manchester, New Hampshire*. He was helpful and forthcoming with Grace Metalious information. Fellow Bookmen Ray Boas and Richard Mori helped me out immensely.

This project would have been impossible without all the local historical society staff workers who answered my calls for help. They are all volunteers. They love the work they do, and it shows.

FOREWORD

Gary Crooker has been around good stories all his life. A longtime antiquarian bookseller, Crooker has spent endless hours searching for titles and authors throughout New Hampshire. That dogged determination led to a fascination with the number of writers either based in the Granite State or influenced by this sometimes harsh, stony environment. This, in turn, was the genesis of the book you are now holding.

This is basically a collection of essays, each one explaining the connection each individual author has with New Hampshire.

Some, such as Sarah Josepha Hale of *Mary Had a Little Lamb* and Grace Metalious, author of *Peyton Place*, were native-born. Others, including Bob Montana, of Archie Comics fame, and poet E.E. Cummings, for instance, were expatriates who chose to move here after spending summers in the bucolic landscape. Although Nathaniel Hawthorne never made his home in New Hampshire, he found inspiration for several of his most famous tales in the White Mountains. For those who wish to delve further into the lives of these authors, Crooker has included a "Beyond the Page" section for many of the essays. These will direct readers to various locations where they can experience the same sense of place that inspired the authors. In the north country town of Littleton, for instance, visitors can enjoy Glad Day every second Saturday in June. The celebration centers on the statue of Pollyanna on the library lawn, honoring the upbeat character made famous by Littleton native Eleanor Porter's 1913 novel. Louisa May Alcott lived in Walpole for parts of three years and drew heavily on the time in her book *Little Women*.

Crooker has unearthed other quirky details and oddities about New Hampshire authors. Did you know that Thomas Edison used Sarah Josepha Hale's poem "Mary Had a Little Lamb" as the first words recorded on his newly invented phonograph? Or that Theodor Geisel was born in Springfield, Massachusetts, but that his pen name, Dr. Seuss, was born in Hanover when he was a student at Dartmouth?

And then there is the story of the two Winston Churchills. Everyone knows British prime minister Winston S. Churchill, who led his nation through World War II. Here, Crooker relates the story of Sir Winston and Cornish bestselling author Winston Churchill as the two crossed paths in the early parts of their careers.

Also revealing is the considerable number of female authors represented in the book, notable considering that writing opportunities were heavily skewed toward men during much of the nineteenth and twentieth centuries.

New Hampshire native and longtime antiquarian book dealer, journalist and author Gary Crooker has always had a soft spot for books. When he was growing up in Wilton, his family encouraged his love for reading and writing—and the Red Sox. I was fortunate enough to work with Gary back in the 1990s as a reporter for the *Milford Cabinet*, sometimes teaming up with him to do feature and sports stories in our coverage of the towns of the Souhegan Valley. Those collaborations exposed me to his subtle Yankee wit and sincere interest in people and the community. He has been active in town affairs and served on the Wilton Old Home Days organization for forty-five years. What really shines through his writing is the genuine enthusiasm he has for his subject, making you want to get involved.

As he notes in his present work: "Have fun, get off the beaten path and explore New Hampshire."

You'll be glad you did.

Joe Adamowicz is the author of *The New Hiking the Monadnock Region: 44 Nature Walks and Day-Hikes in the Heart of New England* and *Johnny Appleseed Hikes for Kids*.

INTRODUCTION

Depending on your perspective, this book took me about seven months or seventy years to write.

From the time I signed a contract with The History Press until I was able to deliver the final project was about a seven-month interval. The aid and guidance provided by the editors at the press have made the book a much less stressful and more enjoyable process throughout.

The seventy-year timeline came about because of many people earlier in my life. I guess I could safely say the existence of this book is largely due to my parents. Dad was a plumber, and Mom was a housewife who worked outside the home when she could for extra cash. Neither was a particularly avid reader—highly intelligent, just not the bookish type. And yet they could not have been more supportive of my love of reading and writing and books from the time I first began to make sense of those little squiggles on the page. Let's just say that my major eleven-year-old love was baseball, but when weather necessitated staying inside to read at recess instead, I wasn't all that disappointed. Thanks, folks; I'm grateful for your support every day. I guess next in line would be public school teachers, public libraries and my colleagues and customers in the antiquarian book trade.

Combined, those were the people and institutions that brought me to this book. I have written it from the point of view of a lifelong reader and longtime antiquarian book dealer. As a former vice president and thirty-five-year member of the New Hampshire Antiquarian Book Association, I have spent a lot of time searching for titles and authors throughout my home state. The more I searched, the more I learned and became intrigued by the number of New Hampshire–based or –influenced authors that existed. Some of the connections, such as Robert Frost, Celia Thaxter, Thomas Bailey Aldrich and Winston Churchill, I was at least partially aware of. Others with significant Granite State connections, such as Willa Cather, Louisa May Alcott, E.E. Cummings and Helen Dore Boylston, I discovered in my travels and built on that as the years went along.

So, from this point of view of a lifetime reader and bookseller, I have tried to put together a literary travelogue for my fellow New Hampshire book lovers. I have always considered my home state to be a day-tripper's delight, and that is every bit as true when following a bookish path. While I recommend that travelers break these trips up into many weeks of discovery, it is possible to jump around quickly due to the short distances between attractions. If desired, one could start in the north country of Littleton appreciating the good vibes of Eleanor Porter and her Pollyanna character. Following that, a trip to the seacoast to experience the Portsmouth of Thomas Bailey Aldrich and Celia Thaxter would be just a two-and-a-half-hour ride. From there, it would take under two hours to be in Jaffrey, visiting the town where Willa Cather produced much of her best work. Although I think the journey is better in smaller bites, you can do it any way you wish. There are no rules for these excursions, just some suggestions and signposts. Following are a few:

First, not a rule but a quite strong suggestion: Check ahead about hours of operation and health regulations in place before making visits. At this writing, COVID-19 rules seem to be easing, but every museum and display handles things differently, so better safe than sorry.

Where appropriate, I have added a "Beyond the Page" section at the end of many of these essays to point the way for travelers. Pollyanna Glad Days in Littleton, the Thomas Bailey Aldrich House in Portsmouth and a trip to the Isle of Shoals to soak up some of the atmosphere that so inspired Celia Thaxter are a few examples.

Another suggestion is to let serendipity be your guide. When my wife (who has been my constant and patient copilot on most of these trips) and I were in Rye Harbor State Park to take photos of the historical markers there, we didn't just snap and run. About forty-five minutes of searching the rocky coast in Rye turned up a handful of sea glass for my wife's craft projects. Likewise for our trip to the Isle of Shoals a couple of hours later. If you like to arrive early at your destinations (as we do) and you enjoy walking historic areas (as we do), you could share our experience. Showing up an hour before our ship was to depart, we traveled some of the narrow and ancient streets of Portsmouth for a forty-five-minute self-guided tour.

There is just so much to see. I would strongly suggest that even if there is no museum or statue or marker associated with a particular author, take time to absorb the sense of place that helped to inspire them.

Lovers of Mount Monadnock often cite the mountain's claim to be one of the most climbed in North America. I would nominate it to also be in the running for the most literary mount. Willa Cather, Elizabeth Yates and all residents of the MacDowell Colony through the years had clear views of Monadnock as they went about their creative days. Ralph Waldo Emerson, Henry David Thoreau, Mark Twain, Nathaniel Hawthorne and Rudyard Kipling all spent time on and/or in the shadow of what Emerson dubbed the New Olympus. All sang its praises.

Mount Chocorua on the easternmost point of the Sandwich Range has a similar pedigree. While Monadnock might be the most climbed, Chocorua could be the most painted, inspiring hundreds of artists through the years. Chocorua's literary credentials are impressive also, with Wallace Stevens and Ezra Pound among the writers who have produced works inspired by the mountain.

Of course, the White Mountain Range has also been the subject of many literary lights. While Eleanor Porter actually grew up in the mountains, many others were inspired by them. Nathaniel Hawthorne, Sarah Orne Jewett and Thoreau all experienced with awe the granite landmarks.

New Hampshire's seacoast highly influenced works by Aldrich, Thaxter and many others. Traveling the state's short but beautiful coastline is a joy in and of itself for literary wanderers. Again, soak up the sense of place that these writers found so appealing. Have fun, get off the beaten path and discover literary New Hampshire.

Finally, take time while visiting some of the destinations mentioned in this guide to appreciate the volunteers who do so much to make them enjoyable and accessible. They may be the folks who are showing you around the grounds or guiding you through the Baldwin Library following a MacDowell Medal Day ceremony. It could be the friendly workers at the Fells in Newbury who make certain they are knowledgeable about every aspect of John Hay's life and career to assist visitors in navigating the house and grounds. Strawbery Banke, Littleton's Pollyanna Glad Days and dozens of local historical societies throughout the state are equally dependent on hardworking volunteers. Theirs is truly a labor of love, and they compound the enjoyment for the rest of us.

Readers may disagree with some of my choices for this book. Some will feel there are writers here who don't belong or that some who do belong have been left out. That's the way it goes when you draw up lists. If this guide provokes that much thought and discussion, I will count it a success.

Enjoy the trip.

PART I

SULLIVAN, CHESHIRE, MERRIMACK AND HILLSBOROUGH COUNTIES

NEW HAMPSHIRE COUNTIES

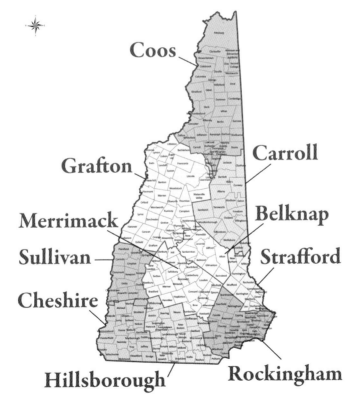

Map of New Hampshire showing counties and towns. *Das.nh.gov.*

Chapter 1

MACDOWELL

Peterborough

Marian Nevins MacDowell, wife of American composer Edward MacDowell, once admitted, "I had the bad but useful habit of not consulting my husband…to follow an impulse and then talk it over with him." Her impulsiveness turned out to be the beginning of one of America's first artist-in-residency programs. The "Peterborough Idea" is still going strong after 115 years.

In 1907, already renowned composer Edward MacDowell and his wife, Marian, deeded their four-hundred-acre Hillcrest Farm in Peterborough to the newly formed Edward MacDowell Association. So began what became the Edward MacDowell Colony Artists in Residence program. In its 115 years of existence since then, MacDowell has seen the creation of hundreds of award-winning works from across the spectrum of artistic disciplines.

The MacDowells purchased the farm on High Street as a summer home in 1896. Marian saw it as a place that would nurture her husband's creative spirit. Undeniably one of the nation's preeminent composers, MacDowell was reluctant about the new property in the beginning. But he told his wife to go ahead and purchase it "with your money." In very short order, he discovered that the High Street property did indeed enable him to do his best work. A log cabin his wife had built for him sealed the deal. Edward MacDowell realized that the solitude of the cabin/studio was a boon to both his output and creativity. It was here that he produced his Woodland

Star Studio cabin, MacDowell. Funded by the Alpha Chi Omega fraternity, Star Studio was the first studio at MacDowell funded by an outside organization. *Postcard image.*

Sketches, Op. 51 for piano. It also planted in him the wish to extend that advantage to other creative artists.

When MacDowell passed away in 1908, Marian took it upon herself to make the vision they both shared into a reality. In addition to attracting prominent names to her fundraising efforts, she resumed her once-promising career as a pianist. Marian took on a series of concerts interpreting her husband's works. Through its first twenty-five formative years, she headed up the nonprofit Edward MacDowell Association.

Today, thirty-two artists' studios dot the landscape and have been used by over eight thousand fellows awarded spots at the retreat. A recent partial count credits residents at MacDowell with over eighty Pulitzer Prizes, thirty-one National Book Awards, thirty Tonys and fifteen Grammys. Some of the better-known residents who have worked at MacDowell include Aaron Copeland, Leonard Bernstein, Thornton Wilder, Willa Cather and Alice Walker.

In 2020, the board of directors dropped the word *colony* from the title of the retreat in an effort to remove "terminology with oppressive overtones."

Whatever changes have come to MacDowell over the years, a very good case can be made that no single place on planet Earth has been responsible for more creative output in the past century than 100 High Street in Peterborough.

BEYOND THE PAGE

MacDowell Medal Day

The purpose explained in the opening of the MacDowell mission statement is "to nurture the arts by offering talented individuals an inspiring residential environment in which to produce enduring works of creative imagination." The solitude extended to the fellows in the program obviously precludes the public from having much access to the grounds. That changes somewhat on MacDowell Medal Day. The MacDowell Medal was established in 1960 and is awarded each year to an individual who has made an outstanding contribution to American culture. The award ceremony typically takes place in June or July; watch the MacDowell website for the date.

The first winner, Thornton Wilder, contributed not only to American culture as a whole but to local culture as well. His 1938 Pulitzer Prize–winning play *Our Town* drew heavily for both characters and settings on Peterborough and surrounding towns in the Monadnock region.

Following the award presentation and a picnic lunch, all visitors are given some access to the grounds and some of the artists' cabins. We attended in 2022 to watch poet Sonia Sanchez receive the honors. One highlight of the tour not to be missed is the James Baldwin Library. Dedicated in 2019, the library contains works of the fellows from MacDowell's 115-year history. Baldwin himself was a resident in 1954, 1957 and 1960.

Historical Marker No. 206: The MacDowell Graves

Located on High Street in Peterborough just before the grounds of MacDowell is New Hampshire Historical Marker No. 206. As it is for so many creative people attracted to the area, Mount Monadnock is a presence that seems to run through the MacDowells' work. Edward and Marian

MacDowell grave markers. New Hampshire Historical Marker No. 206 marks the graves of Edward and Marian MacDowell on High Street in Peterborough. *Melissa Crooker photograph.*

MacDowell chose to rest eternally within sight of the mountain, as the marker explains:

> Buried on this site are noted composer Edward MacDowell (1860–1909) and his wife, Marian Nevins MacDowell (1857–1956). The composer often paused at this boulder to watch the sun set behind Mount Monadnock. Edward and Marian purchased a small farm and moved to Peterborough in 1896. Together they founded the MacDowell Colony in 1907, the first and leading residency program for artists in the United States. The MacDowell Colony continues to offer talented artists ideal working conditions in which they can produce enduring works of imagination.

Chapter 2

WILELLA SIBERT CATHER

1873–1947
Jaffrey

For a native-born book lover, I came to the New Hampshire connection of Willa Cather rather late. Not to Cather's works, mind you—just to what a strong connection she actually had to the Granite State. As far as her actual writings, I have had cause to turn to them often.

At one time, my local library had a tradition of setting aside an evening each December for interested citizens to come in and share a favorite piece of holiday literature with their neighbors. I always took part, and over the years, I read from Kenneth Grahame, Dylan Thomas, Pearl Buck and a few others. But my favorite passage, which I read several years, was from chapter 12 of Cather's *My Ántonia*. In that scene, Ántonia's stern and often unyielding father is faced with the prospect of sharing a prayer with a neighbor of a differing religious persuasion at a Christmas gathering. When Ántonia expresses concern about her father's possible reaction, he responds with a most seasonally appropriate, "It is alright, the prayers of all good men are good."

So much for Willa and me. Now, my fellow Granite Staters, on to Willa Cather and us. Wilella Sibert Cather was born in Virginia in 1873, and her family moved to Nebraska when she was just nine years old. Her life there until she graduated from the University of Nebraska in 1895 provided the background for her Prairie Trilogy of *O Pioneers!* (1913), *The Song of the Lark* (1915) and *My Ántonia* (1918). By virtue of these three novels alone, Cather stands securely as one of the great chroniclers of the American Midwest.

Above: Grave site of Willa Cather and her companion Edith Lewis in Jaffrey's Old Burying Ground. Cather died of a stroke in 1947 at the age of seventy-three. *Melissa Crooker photograph.*

Opposite: The Shattuck Inn in Jaffrey, where novelist Willa Cather spent many seasons and created much of her best work. *Postcard image.*

Published by Duncan, The Druggist, Inc.   Shattuck Inn, Jaffrey, N. H.   Hand Colored

After so much time relying on the fictional works of Willa Cather for my own needs and enjoyment, I happened on to her presence here in the Granite State. While working on a monthly column I used to write on books, it came to my attention that one of my favorite writers did some of her best and most important work right here in Jaffrey, New Hampshire. It was such an important location in her life that by her own direction, she was buried in Jaffrey's Old Burying Ground.

But let's start at the beginning. Cather and her friend Edith Lewis first came to Jaffrey in 1917, visiting friends at the Shattuck Inn at the base of Mount Monadnock. She would return yearly for many seasons, working in her room at the inn or in a nearby field called High Mowing. That work would include some of her very best.

Much of the finishing stages of *My Ántonia* were completed in Jaffrey. In addition, her World War I novel *One of Ours* drew heavily on her time in Jaffrey. Local doctor Frederick Sweeney had recently completed service in the war. Cather overcame the doctor's reluctance and convinced him to let her use his diary for background. The story originated from the very real death overseas of her cousin G.P. Cather. That very close-to-home war experience, along with Dr. Sweeney's diary, were combined by Cather into the winner of the 1923 Pulitzer Prize for fiction.

In 1928, Cather and Lewis began summering on Grand Manan Island in New Brunswick's Bay of Fundy. Despite their new summer haunt, Cather returned to Jaffrey for many autumns. She spent time writing, hiking Mount Monadnock and interacting with local friends made over the years. Despite all the wonderful prose produced during her time in the area, she referred to the Shattuck as her "old resting place."

As noted earlier, Cather also chose Jaffrey as her eternal resting place. Willa Cather and her longtime friend and confidant Edith Lewis are buried in the same plot in Jaffrey's Old Burying Ground. The site provides visitors with a wonderful view of the mountain they both loved. Her gravestone inscription further solidifies her philosophy of life and literature. From *My Ántonia*: "That is happiness; to be dissolved into something complete and great."

BEYOND THE PAGE

The very active Jaffrey Historical Society maintains several files on Willa Cather and her time in town that can be accessed by appointment for anyone interested. The phone number for the society is 603-598-0120, where you may leave a message.

The Shattuck Inn, where Willa Cather spent so much enjoyable as well as productive time, is gone, but the views she reveled in remain. They can be viewed from the Dublin Road Taproom and Eatery on the former site. Also still there is the Shattuck Golf Course, offering the same scenic vistas.

The bucolic setting of Willa Cather's gravestone in the Old Burying Ground is located behind the Meeting House. The address for the Meeting House is 15 Laban Ainsworth Way in Jaffrey. Just a short walk away in the same burying ground you will find the grave of another famous Jaffrey resident by the name of Amos Fortune, and that will make for a very smooth segue to our next New Hampshire writer.

Chapter 3

ELIZABETH YATES McGREAL

1905–2001
Peterborough

During my years in the antiquarian book business, I have dealt with many people who collect specific types of books on specific subjects. One of the best and most popular methods of building a collection of books is to center on all the works of a particular author. It doesn't need to be a world-famous author. Let me give you an example.

I only met Peterborough's Elizabeth Yates McGreal once. It might even be a stretch to call it a meeting, as I was just one of many who heard her speak at an event and then stood in line to have her sign a book. I don't collect her books, but I guess over the years they have collected me, as I have gone on meeting her over a lifetime of reading.

Elizabeth was a joy to meet in her book *My Diary—My World*. In this diary covering her formative years, she relates her story of a privileged but disciplined upbringing in Buffalo, New York, where she was born in 1905. Her later life as a lover of animals and the written word are presaged in its pages. So, too, is her belief in the ability of an individual to break with the past and create their own future. Her natural curiosity and love of nature come through as readers get to witness her develop the themes that recur in over fifty titles over her writing career.

I have met Elizabeth in her 1951 Newbury Award–winning title *Amos Fortune, Free Man*. Amos Fortune was a talented tanner who lived and worked in Jaffrey and is buried there in the Old Burying Ground in the same final resting place as author Willa Cather. The inscription on his grave marker reads, "Sacred to the memory of Amos Fortune, who was born free in Africa, a slave in America, he purchased Liberty, professed Christianity, Lived reputably and died Hopefully November 17 1801 aged 91." From that short inscription, Elizabeth Yates started at the end and worked her way to the beginning as she crafted Amos Fortune's story. The manner in which she told that story has educated generations of young readers about slavery and freedom in a way no textbook could.

Telling other folks' stories was a particular strength of Elizabeth Yates. That talent is on display in the pages of her 1966 book *Is There a Doctor in the Barn?* Readers are brought along on a day in the life of local veterinarian Dr. Forrest Tenney. Yates combines her love of animals, her natural storytelling talents and her respect for a life of accomplishments as she follows her neighbor's travels. It is a nice two-for-one deal, as you get to meet both Yates and Tenney, a pair of Peterborough legends.

Follow Elizabeth Yates on a journey through 1973's *The Road Through Sandwich Notch*. The book has been credited with helping to prevent the natural area from development. Sandwich Notch was eventually incorporated into the White Mountain National Forest and is still available for all to enjoy. There are many who are responsible for preservation of Sandwich Notch, but Elizabeth Yates is certainly one who is owed a debt of gratitude.

The sign marking the entrance to the Shieling Forest grounds, originally the home of Elizabeth Yates McGreal and William McGreal in Peterborough. *Melissa Crooker photograph.*

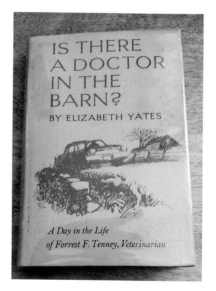

Is There a Doctor in the Barn?, Elizabeth Yates's story of a day in the life of Peterborough veterinarian Forrest Tenney. *Gary Crooker photograph.*

I have described just a few of the places where I have had the pleasure of meeting Elizabeth Yates McGreal: in her diary, through the lives of Amos

Fortune and Doc Tenney and along the road through Sandwich Notch. There are many other places where readers can find her and she can find them. In addition to her books, she authored articles for many magazines. In all of them, her philosophy and personality shine through.

Elizabeth even arranged to bring visitors into her home by way of her writing. When she and her husband moved into their home in Peterborough, renovations uncovered beautiful stenciling left by a previous owner. Elizabeth turned the discovery into the book *Patterns on the Wall*. It is the tale of an itinerant painter who faces unfair persecution as he attempts to ply his trade in early America. Again, justice and redemption seem to run through this story.

So if by chance you haven't met her yet, I'm glad to be the one to provide your introduction to Elizabeth Yates. With apologies to Humphrey Bogart and Claude Rains, "I think this is the beginning of a beautiful friendship."

BEYOND THE PAGE

Follow up a visit to the Old Burying Ground in Jaffrey to the grave site of Willa Cather by proceeding to the upper end of the same yard. There you will find the final resting place of Amos Fortune and his wife, with the poignant inscription that inspired Elizabeth Yates's award-winning book.

No place preserves the legacy of Elizabeth Yates and her husband, William McGreal, better than the Shieling Forest at 395 Old Street in Peterborough. It was previously the residence of the McGreals, and Elizabeth donated the

The stones of Amos Fortune and his wife, Violet, in Jaffrey's Old Burying Ground. From these, Elizabeth Yates wove her Newbury-winning book, *Amos Fortune, Free Man. Melissa Crooker photograph.*

buildings and forty-seven acres of land to the State of New Hampshire. Hiking trails, educational programs and a Forestry Learning Center are all part of the Shieling Forest. For more information, contact the Community Forestry and Stewardship Bureau–Urban Forestry Center at 45 Elwyn Road, Portsmouth, NH, 03801-5701, telephone 603-431-6774.

The Sandwich Notch Road that Elizabeth Yates was so instrumental in preserving is a nine-mile stretch running from Thornton to Center Sandwich that will provide visitors and hikers the same experiences and views that Elizabeth Yates describes in her book. The road is usually closed for the winter but reopens around May depending on weather conditions. The one-lane gravel route can be driven but only by vehicles with high ground clearance. Visitors might want to check with the Sandwich Police Department to verify the status of the road in advance.

Chapter 4

EDNA DEAN PROCTOR

1829–1923
Henniker

She was one of a kind, just like Henniker, the town where she was born and raised.

Edna Dean Proctor was one of America's most popular poets from the Civil War era through the early years of the twentieth century. Her ultra-patriotic Union poems and her nostalgic New Hampshire Old Home Day poetry cemented her popularity as a top literary figure of her day. And it all started, as the town website proudly proclaims, in "the Only Henniker on Earth."

Proctor was born in Henniker in 1829 to John and Lucinda Proctor. Except for an illness-shortened stint at Mount Holyoke Seminary, she received the bulk of her formal education in the town of her birth and neighboring Concord.

It was her stirring poetry during the Civil War that made Proctor the darling of the Union troops. Although little noted today, her poems were a staple of both the campfires and the home fires during the war. "The Stars and Stripes" (April 1861), "Compromise" (July 1861) and "Who's Ready" (July 1862) were all prime examples of her craft accurately aimed at keeping morale high at the battlefront as well as the home front. The latter, penned in 1862 when the fortunes of the Confederates were high, was typical, with lines like "God help us! Who's ready? There's danger before! Who's armed who's mounted? The foes at the door." Neither her sense of urgency nor her use of exclamation points to express it wavered throughout the conflict.

Proctor was no latecomer to the cause of abolition and the preservation of the Union. In 1850, she met Harriet Beecher Stowe. Proctor became an acolyte of Harriet's brother Henry Ward Beecher. She copied down his sermons, many filled with his fiercely antislavery opinions, from the years 1856 through 1858. She later published them under the title *Life Thoughts Gathered from the Extemporaneous Discourses of Henry Ward Beecher*.

The Civil War came to an end in 1865, but Edna Dean Proctor and her literary contributions still had a way to go. Though initially known and respected for her poetry, in the postwar era, she branched out into a prose career that won her accolades from fellow writers. Immediately following the end of the war, she traveled extensively with the Charles Storrs family, fellow abolitionist-leaning friends from Brooklyn. They visited Europe, the Middle East and the Holy Land. The major work to come out of her journals from these voyages was 1890's *A Russian Journey*. Henry Wordsworth Longfellow and John Greenleaf Whittier expressed great enthusiasm for both the book and author.

Despite her love of travel and her success as a travel writer, Edna Dean Proctor always held a place in her heart for both the town and the state of her birth. Her rural New Hampshire upbringing was often reflected in the imagery of her work. In 1899, when Governor Frank Rollins declared the first Old Home Week Celebrations in the state, Proctor was tabbed to

Proctor Square in Henniker, named after poet Edna Dean Proctor by a grateful community. *Postcard image.*

Henniker's arch bridge seemed to be totally destroyed by this damage from the 1938 hurricane. Funds left by Edna Dean Proctor were used to fully restore the bridge, which is now named for her. *Postcard image.*

produce "The Hills Are Home" as the first official poem of the newly minted holiday. In 1900, *The Mountain Maid and Other Poems of New Hampshire* again reiterated her fondness for the hills of her youth.

BEYOND THE PAGE

Henniker's gift to the world of literature provided for her hometown even beyond her time on earth. Her will left funds for a fountain to be constructed in Proctor Square in Henniker. The will also left monies for the maintenance of the stone arch bridge in town that spanned her beloved Contoocook River. When the bridge sustained serious damage from a 1938 hurricane, repairs were provided using the money from those funds. The Town of Henniker renamed it the Edna Dean Proctor Bridge.

Chapter 5

HENRY DENMAN THOMPSON

1833–1911

Swanzey

Henry Denman Thompson wasn't the most prolific of authors connected to New Hampshire. He did, however, produce several plays. One, *The Old Homestead*, which is based on his time in Swanzey, had an incredible run in that town.

Thompson's *The Old Homestead* opened in Boston in 1886 and made him a wealthy man. He toured the country with the sentimental story of country life and values and used the proceeds to build a farm and cottage in Swanzey, where he had lived during his childhood.

Many years of travel and work involving the theater followed Thompson's childhood in Swanzey. He worked rather unsuccessfully as a dramatic actor, moving on to more moderate success in comedy and vaudeville.

It was while with a vaudeville troupe that Thompson produced a short piece about Joshua Whitcomb. The character was portrayed as a country rube who comes to the city. Starting in 1875, Thompson performed the short, humorous piece himself on stage. Audiences loved it. Thompson quite shrewdly gave them even more to love. He expanded the sketch into a four-act play called *The Old Homestead*. As mentioned, the 1886 Boston opening of the play made Thompson's fortune, with which he constructed the farm and cottage in Swanzey where he lived for the rest of his life. The play made Broadway in 1905, and in 1915, it was made into a silent film.

This was quite a successful run for a small-town boy made good. But the longest run of all was still in the offing. Thompson's tale of Uncle

Denman Thompson, who turned a short vaudeville sketch into *The Old Homestead*. The four-act play ran from 1939 to 2016 in Swanzey's Potash Bowl. *Postcard image.*

Josh's travails in the big city was set in Swanzey, and it was in Swanzey where it played from 1939 to 2016. It was performed in the Potash Bowl, Swanzey's natural amphitheater. The play opened in July 1939 and featured local amateurs; its run entertained thousands. Unfortunately, 2016 brought the curtain down on the Swanzey tradition. Will Uncle Josh and *The Old Homestead* ever return to the Potash Bowl? Who knows? It's hard to keep a good play down.

BEYOND THE PAGE

New Hampshire Historical Marker No. 22 is located just south of New Hampshire Route 32 and Sawyers Crossing Road. It reads:

> *Denman Thompson 1833–1911. A famous theatrical trouper who lived and died in West Swanzey. He gained a national reputation by his portrayal of the character 'Joshua Whitcomb,' the New Hampshire farmer on a trip to Boston. From this he subsequently evolved 'The Old Homestead,' a play of long runs before enthusiastic audiences.*

Chapter 6

SARAH JOSEPHA BUELL HALE

1788–1877

Newport

Make no mistake about it, Newport's Sarah Josepha Hale was a very busy lady for a very long time.

In 1827, at the age of thirty-nine, a full thirty-four years before the start of the Civil War, she wrote one of the first American novels dealing with the issue of slavery in the United States. Fifty years later, in 1877, she retired from *Godey's Lady's Book* after a career as one of the most successful magazine editors in history. Just four months prior to her retirement, Thomas Edison used her wildly popular poem "Mary Had a Little Lamb" as the first words recorded on his newly invented phonograph. She saw and made a lot of history in her ninety years.

She was born Sarah Josepha Buell in 1788 to parents who believed more in education for women than was common at the time. She nonetheless had only homeschooling from her mother and brother before she married local lawyer David Hale in 1813. They had five children together, but her husband passed away in 1822, forcing the still-young widow to change course in her life and embark on an independent career to support her family.

Consider what a career it turned out to be.

With the 1830 publication of Hale's first book of poetry, "Mary Had a Little Lamb" became one of the most popular poems written. It was based on an actual incident that took place during Hale's time as a schoolteacher. It has been recited by young students ever since and, as aforementioned, was used by Thomas Edison to test his phonograph.

Hale was the first president of the Seaman's Aid Society of the city of Boston. This women's aid society operated as a boardinghouse for sailors and a school for their children. The organization merged with the Boston Port Society in 1867 and operated as the Boston Port and Seamen's Society until 1977.

In 1827, Hale authored her novel *Northwood, or, Life North and South: Showing the True Character of Both*. It was one of the first antislavery novels to be published. The book received mostly positive reviews in the North and was favorably viewed by the Reverend John Lauris Blake, who owned *Ladies* magazine and convinced Sarah to come to Boston to work as the publication's editor. The magazine was purchased in 1837 by Louis Godey, and the name changed to *Godey's Lady's Book*.

Over her fifty-year career as a magazine editor, Hale was influential in the political and literary scenes of the day. She tirelessly promoted the cause of female education (though not suffrage). In addition, she nurtured the careers of what were to become many of the major talents in American fiction and poetry. With far and away the largest circulation of any publication of the sort, *Godey's Lady's Book* listed among its contributors Lydia Sigourney, Frances Sargent Osgood, Oliver Wendell Holmes, Nathaniel Hawthorne, Washington Irving and Edgar Allan Poe, to name a few. Not a bad stable of writing talent, but by no means the end of Hale's accomplishments.

The daughter of a Revolutionary War officer, Hale took charge when efforts to raise money for the erection of the Bunker Hill Monument seemed to be coming to a standstill. The Bunker Hill Monument Association had been formed, but the initial flow of funds was down to a trickle. Enter Sarah Josepha Hale. Using the pulpit of her *Godey's* editorship, she promoted a women's fair to raise the money needed. Heavily promoted by *Godey's*, the fair was held at Boston's Faneuil Hall, selling food, needlework and crafts. The six-day fair raised over $33,000, more than was needed to complete construction of the monument. Under Hale, the pages of *Godey's* were similarly employed in the successful efforts to preserve George Washington's Mount Vernon home.

In keeping with her lifelong commitment to furthering the educational opportunities offered to women, Hale was an early and frequent supporter of Vassar College. From the time of its charter in 1861, she was in frequent contact with founder Matthew Vassar. Both personally and through the pages of *Godey's*, she promoted the college throughout her time as editor.

Sarah Josepha Hale was one of the most prominent and effective national editors of her time. She composed one of the most iconic nursery rhymes

Opposite, top: New Hampshire Historical Marker No. 6, detailing the life and works of Newport's Sarah Josepha Hale. *Melissa Crooker photograph.*

Opposite, bottom: Plaque located in Sarah Josepha Hale Memorial Park outlining the components of the park's tributes to Newport's most famous native. *Melissa Crooker photograph.*

Above: The main bust in the Sarah Josepha Hale Memorial Park depicting one of the nineteenth century's leading editors and the "Mother of Thanksgiving." *Melissa Crooker photograph.*

of all time. She was a major promoter and supporter of some of the most famous names in American literature. Despite all those credentials and more, she may, after all, be best remembered as the person who created a national holiday.

Hale lobbied for many causes as editor of *Godey's* but none more enthusiastically and, eventually, successfully as the establishment of a national day of thanksgiving. There were certainly many proponents of such a holiday before Hale, but as might be expected, it was her tenacity that won the day. That tenacious attitude finally bore fruit (as well as turkey, gravy and stuffing) when her direct appeals to President Abraham Lincoln resulted in Presidential Proclamation 118, which designated a national day of thanksgiving. From that day forward, Sarah Josepha Hale, from Newport, New Hampshire, became known as the Mother of Thanksgiving.

BEYOND THE PAGE

The first places to visit when you arrive at the hometown of Sarah Josepha Hale are the Newport Historical Society and Museum at 20 Central Street and the Richards Free Library at 58 North Main Street. Both have materials pertaining to their town's famous daughter and folks who are friendly and willing to talk about her. The Historical Society and Museum is open on Sundays from 10:00 a.m. to 2:00 p.m. The contact number is 603-863-1294. The Richards Free Library is open on Mondays 1:00–6:00 p.m.; Tuesday, Wednesday and Thursday 10:00 a.m.–8:00 p.m.; Friday 10:00 a.m.–6:00 p.m.; and Saturday 10:00 a.m.–2:00 p.m.

Also on the grounds of the Richards Free Library, a must visit is the Sarah Josepha Buell Hale Memorial Park. In addition to the bust of Hale by Finnish sculptor Jari Männistö, the display includes arms with broken shackles as a nod to her antislavery work. Also included is a plaque that recounts her many works of historical and literary importance. In 2013, the site was designated a Literary Landmark in celebration of the 150th anniversary of the Thanksgiving holiday.

Located, appropriately enough, on Hale Street is New Hampshire Historical Marker No. 6, which reads as follows: Sarah Josepha Hale, "Prominent humanitarian, poet and author was born and taught school in the Guild section of Newport. Widowed mother of five, she edited 'Godey's Lady's Book,' 1837–1877; composed poem now called 'Mary Had a Little Lamb'; advocated proclamation of Thanksgiving Day as a national festival; and appealed constantly for higher education for women."

The Sarah Josepha Hale Award was established in 1956 and is presented each year to a writer with a significant body of work who is from or has had a notable association with New England. Robert Frost was the first recipient of the award. Others include Elizabeth Yates, Tomie dePaola and Ernest Hebert.

Chapter 7

WINSTON CHURCHILL

1871–1947
Cornish

W hen I first opened an antiquarian bookshop back in the 1990s, it was located on the main street of Wilton, New Hampshire. Main Street is also the location of a very successful movie theater, so on weekends I would stay open late in an effort to catch the crowds coming out of the movies.

One Friday, my business strategy worked pretty well. Several browsers dropped in after the late show let out. One young couple seemed particularly enthusiastic about their choices, commenting that they "never knew he had written these books" and "he must have authored them when he was much younger." To make a long story less long, they had come across books by Cornish, New Hampshire novelist and political figure Winston Churchill and mistaken his works for those of his now much more famous namesake, Sir Winston Churchill. While the pile of books looked like a nice sale, I, of course, had to explain their mistake. It turned out happily for all involved, as they proceeded to purchase all the books in their pile as they found the story of the two Winstons so interesting.

See if you agree.

The Winston Churchill of New Hampshire fame was born in St. Louis in 1871. While he is overshadowed today in the public eye by the British statesman, he became quite accomplished early in his life. He graduated from the United States Naval Academy in 1894, and in his time, he was a standout in fencing and crew.

But instead of a lifetime naval career, Churchill launched a writing life that eventually landed him in New Hampshire. After a short stint as managing editor at *Cosmopolitan Magazine*, full-time writing called, and almost immediately, he became one of the twentieth century's most popular novelists. In 1898, his first novel in book form, *The Celebrity*, appeared and was a moderate success. In 1899, *Richard Carvel*, a Revolutionary War–era historical tale, was published. It reached the bestseller list in 1899 and 1900.

Enter England's Winston Churchill. This might be a good spot to point out the marked similarities between these two unrelated writers. They were quite close in age, with America's Winston just three years older than his namesake. They both came from military backgrounds, both were interested in politics, both liked to paint for relaxation in their spare time and both harbored hopes for literary careers. It indeed seemed like a situation with great potential for confusion. The Winston who was destined to become Sir Winston and a giant of the twentieth century was actually much less well known in 1899. But it was he who expressed his concern in a letter that year. Here, in part, is the first contact between the two, penned in June 1899 from England:

> *Mr. Winston Churchill sends his compliments to Mr. Winston Churchill and begs to draw his attention to a matter which concerns them both. He has learnt from the Press notices that Mr. Winston Churchill proposes to bring out another novel, entitled "Richard Carvel" which is certain to have a considerable sale both in England and America. Churchill is also the author of a novel* [Savrola] *now being published in serial form in MacMillan's Magazine and for which he anticipates some sale both in England and America. He has no doubt that Mr. Winston Churchill will recognize from this letter—if indeed by no other means—that there is a grave danger of his works being mistaken for those of Mr. Winston Churchill. He feels sure that Mr. Winston Churchill desires this as little as he does himself.*

It is at this point, where the letter seems on the verge of turning into an Abbott and Costello routine, that the future Sir Winston proposes his solution to the perceived problem.

> *In the future to avoid mistakes as much as possible, Mr. Winston Churchill has decided to sign all published articles, stories or other work "Winston Spencer Churchill" and not "Winston Churchill" as formerly. He trusts that this arrangement will commend itself to Mr. Winston Churchill.*

As it turned out, the American Winston Churchill did indeed agree to the proposal. Winston Spencer Churchill became the name his British counterpart used going forward, until it was shortened to Winston S. Churchill after a few years. The two did meet a couple of times, once in America and once in England, but never became close acquaintances.

In addition to the transatlantic correspondence between the two Churchills, 1899 also marked the completion in Cornish of Harlakenden House. Named for Churchill's wife, born Mabel Harlakenden, it was the residence of the couple until it was destroyed by fire in 1923. The completion of the home marked the couple's total immersion in the Cornish Art Colony. It was also the site of another of Churchill's brushes with history, as it served as the Summer White House for his friend Woodrow Wilson from 1913 to 1915.

Success as a novelist continued to make his name a familiar one nationwide. The incredible reception of *Richard Carvel* was followed by more dominance of the bestseller list. Following that success, he stuck to the popular historical novel formula. *The Crisis* (1901) returned to his home state of Missouri and covered the period immediately preceding the Civil War and the conflict's early battles. According to *Bookman Magazine*, it was the bestselling book of 1903. His final historical novel, *The Crossing*, tackled the westward expansion of the United States. The winning streak continued as it hit number one on the lists for 1904.

It was also during these early years when Churchill's interest in politics resulted in a term in the New Hampshire legislature from 1903 to 1905. He followed up with an unsuccessful bid for governor as a progressive candidate. Another failed bid for the same office in 1912 brought an end to his political aspirations. Despite his defeats, politics clearly came to play a much larger role in his stories.

Churchill moved on from the grand historical novel and began writing contemporary tales, usually incorporating his brand of progressive political thought. Despite the change, his popularity continued. Published in 1906, *Coniston* is set in New Hampshire with a political theme and is dependent for setting in large part on the real-life town of Croydon, New Hampshire. Croydon's Coniston General Store and 110-acre Lake Coniston are named in recognition of the novel's influence and popularity.

The author switched his approach a final time in his later novels, turning inward—and progressively more didactic—as religion and personal philosophy played larger roles in his storytelling. Starting with *A Modern Chronicle* (1910) and continuing through his final, *The Dwelling-Place of Life* (1917), he continued to sell well.

Top: Village of "Coniston," based on the real town of Croydon, in the time of "Jethro Bass," based on Ruel Durkee, a real nineteenth-century politician. *Postcard image.*

Bottom: Destroyed by fire in 1923, Harlakenden House served as a home for novelist Winston Churchill and his wife as well as the Summer White House of Woodrow Wilson. *Postcard image.*

Opposite: New Hampshire Highway Marker No. 16 tells the story of author Winston Churchill's career and Harlakenden House in Cornish. *Melissa Crooker photograph.*

Of course, all this literary acclaim took place against the backdrop of the Cornish Art Colony. Churchill was acquainted with most of the creative members of the community and was very close with several. His beloved Harlakenden was designed by fellow colonist Charles Platt. He was also close friends with artist Stephen Parrish and his talented son Maxfield.

As quickly as Churchill's storytelling career rocketed, it came to a halt after 1919. Once he decided to stop writing, he receded quickly from the public consciousness. In 1940, he reappeared with *The Uncharted Way*, about his religious thought. It wasn't well publicized and had very low sales. Not long before his death in Winter Park, Florida, Churchill commented, "It is very difficult now for me to think of myself as a writer of novels, as all that seems to belong to another life."

Another life, indeed. But what a life it was. It was one in which he became one of the most successful and well-recognized authors of his time. He graduated from the U.S. Naval Academy and was an occasionally successful and influential politician. He was the friend of presidents and moved the man who became known as "the Lion of the Western World" to change the way he signed his name. Not a bad life at all.

Beyond the Page

New Hampshire Historical Marker No. 16

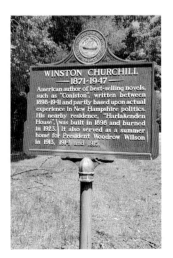

The New Hampshire Historical Marker erected in honor of author Winston Churchill is located on Wilson Road (New Hampshire Route 12A), three-tenths of a mile south of Ferry Crossing Hill Road on the right when traveling south. The marker reads:

Winston Churchill, 1871–1947. American author of best-selling novels, such as "Coniston" written between 1898–1941 and partly based upon actual experience in New Hampshire politics. His nearby residence, "Harlakenden House," was built in 1898 and burned in 1923. It also served as a summer home for President Woodrow Wilson in 1913, 1914 and 1915.

Chapter 8

JEROME DAVID SALINGER

1919–2010
Cornish

While we are on the subject of Cornish, let's jump forward in the century to another famous author who made his home there. I mean, "if you really want to hear about it..."

Salinger moved to Cornish and was a resident from 1953 until his death in 2010. *The Catcher in the Rye*, his classic tale of teenage alienation, was the first and last novel he published, but it certainly had staying power. It was standard reading when I was in high school, and my grandson was assigned it to read just last year.

As far as Salinger's time in New Hampshire goes, Cornish was a good choice. The townspeople already had a long history of celebrities walking among them. With the possible exception of Greta Garbo, no one has ever been more famous than Salinger for wanting to be alone. Cornish residents seemed be fine with that, as they were famously reticent when confronted with inquiries about their famous neighbor.

The race by reporters to stymie Salinger's desire to avoid them became a major narrative during his New Hampshire years. When he was new in town, Salinger spent considerable time with local high school students. But when he granted an interview to a high schooler for the student paper, the story ended up going out to the city press. That proved a turning point in Salinger's interaction with his neighbors.

As far as his writing went, J.D. Salinger did publish some collections during his time in New Hampshire. Nine stories came out in 1953. In addition, writing about young people, which he did a lot, Salinger drew heavily on his combat experiences in World War II. "A Perfect Day for Bananafish" (1948) and "For Esmé—with Love and Squalor" (1950) both appear in *Nine Stories* and are both examples of this. "Raise High the Roof Beam, Carpenters" and "Seymour: An Introduction" were both published in the *New Yorker* during Salinger's years in New Hampshire; the two novellas deal with the saga of the Glass family.

Though most of the attention paid to Salinger while in the Granite State seemed to take the form of fascination with his so-called hermit style of life, he also turned out some of the twentieth century's best prose while here. By all accounts, he was not your run-of-the-mill celebrity, but it was during a time when this was not quite the art form it has become. He was a tremendous writer who even stunned Hemingway with his talent.

And like Garbo, he never said he wanted to be alone, only that he wanted to be left alone.

Chapter 9

CHARLES CARLETON COFFIN

1823–1896

Boscawen

Boscawen native and Civil War correspondent Charles Carleton Coffin has been referred to as the Ernie Pyle of his time. Now, I grew up hearing from my World War II veteran father about the special relationship between reporter Ernie Pyle and the combat soldiers in that war. The quantity and quality of Coffin's reporting from the Civil War front lines would justify the comparison.

But perhaps later generations might look at Coffin's career and see a resemblance not only with Pyle but also with the character Forrest Gump. Just as Gump seems to turn up at nearly every major historical event of his lifetime, the ubiquitous Coffin seemed to jump from one Civil War–era milestone to the next. It was a career that eventually earned him a spot on the Correspondents Memorial Arch in Maryland's Gathland State Park.

A quick glance at Coffin's early life gives little indication that a career as a journalist and author was in the offing. But as often happens in retrospect, events seemed to be pointing that way all along. Born in 1823 in Boscawen, his initial interests seemed to be steering him in different directions. Self-educated in the science of surveying, at twenty-one, he left his rural New Hampshire home behind and put his skills to work with a roadbuilding crew in Boston. Although the work was apparently to his liking, he suffered an axe wound to his ankle that affected his future choices. The highly pro-Union and antislavery Coffin lost his option for soldiering in the coming conflict because of the wound.

The stone and bronze plaque in Boscawen marking the birthplace of Charles Carleton Coffin. It is located in front of Richardson's Orchard and Farm Stand. *Melissa Crooker photograph.*

A job with the Northern Railroad and work on electric power lines connecting Boston and Cambridge all preceded his decision to make a change to what would be his life's true calling. Coffin joined the *Boston Journal* and began the writing career that would define the rest of his working life. It also set him on the path to his Gump-like odyssey through the Civil War. Not only did his talent for human interest stories endear him to readers and soldiers alike, but he also benefited from seeming to always be in the right place at the right time.

Consider his impressive timeline writing under the byline "Carleton."

He was present and reporting at the historic Republican Convention in Chicago that nominated Abraham Lincoln and accelerated the chain of events that would lead to the secession of Southern states and the firing on Fort Sumter.

From Chicago, he joined the group that traveled to Springfield, Illinois, to officially inform Lincoln of his nomination. After that came his reporting on the 1860 campaign and Lincoln's inauguration. Heady stuff, but our intrepid reporter was just getting started.

When the war got underway in earnest, Coffin was right there at the first Battle of Bull Run as the Union troops were routed by the Confederates. He was at Antietam to witness the bloodiest day of battle on American soil. He was at Gettysburg, even accompanying Colonel Joshua Chamberlain on his way to the defense of Little Round Top. Throw in the Battle of the Wilderness and being present when the war came full circle and the American flag was once again raised over Fort Sumter.

Following the end of the war, the small-town-boy-turned-journalist translated his experiences into a stream of related books. Titles such as *My Days and Nights on the Battlefield*, *The Boys of 61* and *Stories of Our Soldiers* were all popular with a reading public eager to hear from a journalist who was there. He never forgot his hometown, either, as he authored *The History of Boscawen and Webster* in 1878.

BEYOND THE PAGE

The Boscawen Historical Society has an extensive collection of Charles Carleton Coffin books. That includes Coffin's 1878 *History of Boscawen and Webster, From 1733 to 1878*. The historical society is located at 226 King Street in the Boscawen Academy School House Building. The museum is open on Sundays 2:00 p.m.–4:00 p.m., May through October. Telephone: 603-975-0111; email: info@boscawenhistoricalsociety.org.

While in Boscawen, also swing by Richardson's Orchard and Farm Stand, located on 170 Water Street. A bronze and stone plaque in front of the stand reads: "Birthplace of Charles Carleton Coffin, Born July 26 AD 1823. Historian of Boscawen, Author, War Correspondent. 'Carleton,' Legislator and Businessman, One who loved and respected his home town."

Chapter 10

JOHN MILTON HAY

1838–1905
Newbury

A s a young man, John Hay of Salem, Indiana, expressed a desire to become a poet and a man of letters as an adult. He is known to history for a long and productive political career. Friend and confidant of presidents from Lincoln to Theodore Roosevelt, his service to his government is rightfully his main claim to fame. But a case can be made that his prolific accomplishments as a statesman in some ways nurtured his career as a writer.

Hay's *Pike County Ballads* was first published in 1871, but the roots of his vernacular poetry reach back to his time in Pittsfield, Illinois. Born in 1838 in Indiana, Hay spent five years living with his uncle Milton Hay from 1850 to 1855. Both before and after the Civil War, Hay mined the dialect of the locale to produce the poetry that was popular in its day.

Those years also produced his relationship with John Nicolay, who served along with Hay as private secretary to Lincoln from the time of his election to his assassination. Friendship and service to the nation's sixteenth president produced a landmark biographical work and permanently linked the names of Hay and Nicolay. The ten-volume *Life of Lincoln* was perhaps the crowning jewel of Hay's writing efforts. The biography, of which Hay is credited with most of the authorship, served as defining account of Lincoln's life for generations.

Hay's time with his uncle was also important in his college education. His uncle's financial support enabled him to study back east at Brown University. Hay made much of the fact that the time there offered him

The main house at the John Hay estate at the Fells. Visitors can tour the twenty-two-room estate from Memorial Day through Columbus Day. *From the Collections of the John Hay Estate at the Fells.*

Listed on the National Register of Historic Places, the Fells includes wonderful views of Lake Sunapee as well as numerous walking trails. *From the Collections of the John Hay Estate at the Fells.*

access to literary friendships and resources that were much superior to those of a western college. He traveled in literary circles while there and was named class poet.

Following Lincoln's death, Hay's political and literary careers continued. His knowledge of Europe was fed by the acceptance of several diplomatic posts. These included serving with the American Legation in Paris and then as a member of the American embassies in Vienna and Madrid. Those post–Civil War duties were accompanied by work as a journalist for the *New York Tribune*. Those experiences along with his service in the State Departments of Presidents Hayes, McKinley and Theodore Roosevelt all aided in his writing of several travel commentaries that were much sought-after and referred to in his time. *Castilian Days*, appearing in 1871, consists of insightful essays on his days in Spain and went through several printings.

With the amount of time John Hay spent in and around political life, it seems inevitable that he would produce a novel of social commentary. That book was *The Bread-Winners*, appearing first in serial form in *Century Magazine* and then in book form in 1884. Written from a pro-capitalist point of view, unlike many novels of the era, it never appeared with Hay listed as author until after his death in 1905.

All this literary output, of course, came as Hay labored as a leading statesman of his time. Besides his four years in the Lincoln White House, he served in differing capacities under Presidents Garfield, Hayes, McKinley and Roosevelt. Seeking respite from the demands of such a life, he began buying up properties in Newbury, New Hampshire, for a summer home, eventually accumulating one thousand acres in the area. He and his wife, Clara Stone Hay, commenced building a summer retreat on the shores of Lake Sunapee. The Fells is named in recognition of Hay's Scottish ancestry. The home remained in the family for three generations. In 1960, the Hay family donated almost seven hundred acres to the Society for the Protection of New Hampshire Forests.

BEYOND THE PAGE

The Fells, 456 Route 103A, Newbury, New Hampshire

Today, the Fells and its 83.5 acres is on the National Register of Historic Places as well as being a preservation project of the Garden Conservancy. Besides about half a mile of Lake Sunapee shoreline, the estate boasts a beautiful array of gardens adjoining the house. Tours of the twenty-two-room house are accompanied by films exploring the life and legacy of John Milton Hay. The main house is open to the public from Memorial Day until Columbus Day. The gardens and trails are open year-round from dawn until dusk. For more information, go to the website https://thefells.org or call 603-763-4789.

Chapter 11

LOUISA MAY ALCOTT

1832–1888
Walpole

Louisa May Alcott's connection with New Hampshire will give readers a chance to visit one of the prettiest towns in the entire state. Walpole, a town author James Michener once described as the "quintessential New England village," was home for Louisa and her family for a couple of years in the mid-1850s and became part of her most famous book.

The Alcotts arrived in Walpole pretty much destitute in 1855. Father Bronson Alcott was a brilliant Utopian thinker, but that Utopian thought did nothing to pay the everyday bills of the family. Those duties fell increasingly on the shoulders of his wife, Abby May, and their older daughters. Louisa's sister Anna arrived in Walpole in 1854 to work as a governess for her cousins. Louisa followed in June 1855, and the remainder of the family came just a month later when Bronson's brother-in-law, Benjamin Willis, offered the family a house rent-free.

Over the next two years, Louisa was back and forth between Boston and Walpole, spending mostly the summer months in Walpole. Many of the experiences related in *Little Women* were actually based on the family's time there. She was also a very active member of the Walpole Amateur Dramatic Company. The years 1855 and 1856 saw her acting in the company's theatricals. She returned for her final summer in 1857 but eventually went back to Concord with financial help from Ralph Waldo Emerson.

Much of what appeared in the 1868 publication of Alcott's *Little Women* was drawn from the family's time in Walpole. In chapter 6, "Beth Finds the

Top: Now the Alcott Apartments, this building on High Street was the home of Louisa May Alcott and her family during their time in Walpole. *Gary Crooker photograph.*

Bottom: Now in the possession of the Walpole Historical Society, this piano was given to Louisa May Alcott by Dr. Henry Bellows. Its story is incorporated into chapter 6 of *Little Women*. *Gary Crooker photograph.*

Palace Beautiful," old Mr. Laurence gifts his granddaughter's piano to Beth. That scene and the piano itself were inspired when Dr. Henry Bellows gave the piano to Louisa May Alcott during her time in Walpole. The actual piano is now in the possession of the Walpole Historical Society.

This information and more came from a nice afternoon with old friend, fellow bookman and Walpole history enthusiast Ray Boas. Besides a tour of the historical society, Ray walked us through town, pointing out the house where the Alcotts lived and several locations where the amateur theatricals took place. It's a walk through the village I would encourage all Louisa May Alcott enthusiasts to take.

Beyond the Page

The Walpole Historical Society maintains a display of memorabilia from Louisa May Alcott's time in town. Included in the display is a woolen petticoat belonging to the author as well as playbills from the performances in which Louisa and her sisters took part. Also on display is the aforementioned piano, which has been totally restored by the society. The society is open Saturdays from noon to 4:00 p.m. and is located at 32 Main Street. The museum is open by appointment. The telephone number for the society is 603-756-3499.

Chapter 12

HARRIET ADAMS WILSON

1825–1900
Milford

To researchers' knowledge, Harriet Wilson's *Our Nig* was the only book she ever published. While Wilson was not nearly as prolific as most of the authors in this book, a case may be made that historically, hers is the most important book of them all. And to think: just forty years ago, neither Wilson nor her novel would even have made the list.

Wilson's book was written in 1859 and, equally importantly, rediscovered in 1981 by Harvard professor Henry Louis Gates Jr. The book was republished in 1981 and has become widely studied and the subject of much literary scrutiny. Thanks to Professor Gates and the Harriet Wilson Project that followed, it has achieved the popularity its author hoped for but failed to attain over 160 years ago.

Born Harriet E. Adams, a free person of color, in Milford in 1825, Wilson was a widowed mother of one son by the time she penned her autobiographical novel. Her son, George, was born in 1852, and Wilson stated she wrote the book to earn money for his care. The book apparently had poor sales, and less than a year after it appeared, George died. It has been speculated that the book had disappointing sales numbers because it didn't fit the mold many northern abolitionists would have hoped for. It was as critical of northern Whites' attitudes toward free Blacks as it was critical of southern whites. That perceived failing was apparent in the book's full title: *Our Nig: or, Sketches from the Life of a Free Black, in a Two-Story White House, North Showing That Slavery's Shadows Fall Even There*. Wilson apparently

Located in Milford's Bicentennial Park, the Harriet E. Wilson memorial commemorates the first African American woman to publish a novel in the United States. *Madeline Carpentiere photograph.*

went on to a life in the Spiritualist community in Boston but never produced another book.

There things stood until Professor Gates and then the Harriet Wilson Project came onto the scene. The rediscovery of the forgotten novel and its establishment as the first by an African American woman in North America started a chain of events. A dispute as to when and at what educational level the teaching of the book was appropriate played out in the local press. Mostly in response to that discussion, The Harriet Wilson Project was formed in 2002. Since then, the group has been active in promoting the reading and study of the book.

Our Nig tells the story of Frado, born to a mixed-race couple and then left in the care of a local family by the name of Bellmont. Frado is put to work and cruelly treated by the family until she turns eighteen and is able to go out on her own. Even then, her struggles continue, as she tries to find her way in a mostly White world.

One of the Harriet Wilson Project's main stated goals at inception was to "orchestrate the creation of a memorial monument for the town of Milford." That goal came to fruition in 2006 when a statue sculpted by artist Fern Cunningham was dedicated in Milford's Bicentennial Park.

Today, Wilson's *Our Nig* has taken its rightful place with other historic literary firsts. It is a tale of the injustice meted out through indentured servitude in the heart of the "abolitionist North." It is a frank denunciation of much of the racism that existed even among those outside the southern states. Perhaps sales were weak because of just that message. But like any worthwhile message, its time eventually came.

BEYOND THE PAGE

The statue commemorating Harriet Wilson, America's first African American novelist, states simply "Harriet Wilson 1825–1900 Author." The monument is located in Milford's Bicentennial Park at 123 South Street. More information on the Harriet Wilson Project can be found at www.harrietwilsonproject.org or by calling 617-539-6886.

Chapter 13

DONALD HALL AND JANE KENYON

1928–2018 and 1947–1995
Wilmot

Donald Hall could have had me at "baseball." The great New Hampshire and United States poet laureate loved the game and wrote and talked of it often. That alone would have won me over. But of course, Hall and his poet wife, Jane Kenyon, both had so much more to offer from Eagle Pond Farm in Wilmot.

The two met when Kenyon was a student in a class taught by Hall at the University of Michigan. In 1972, they married. In 1975, the couple moved to Wilmot. For over two decades there at the ancestral home of Hall's family, they brought to New Hampshire and the world their love story along with an inspiring burst of creativity.

From 1975 until the far too early death of Jane Kenyon in 1995, the poetic couple shared the home where Donald Hall had spent many of his summers as a boy. Kenyon produced four volumes of her spare and introspective poetry filled with the rural images that surrounded her at Eagle Pond. *From Room to Room* (1978), *The Boat of Quiet Hours* (1986), *Let Evening Come* (1990) and *Constance* (1993) were all published in her lifetime. Greater poetry experts than I have examined and critiqued Kenyon's poetry, but for my money, it would be difficult to find a better poem than "Let Evening Come." The title poem of her 1990 collection is particularly poignant in view of her death just five years later from leukemia. The imagery and message of acceptance and balance in life are unmistakable and presented in the simple form that was her trademark. Jane Kenyon was the winner of the 1994 PEN/Voelcker

Left: The Eagle Pond Farmhouse, where Donald Hall spent youthful summers with his grandparents. Hall's book *String Too Short to Be Saved* was his paean to those summers. *Melissa Crooker photograph.*

Right: The barn at Eagle Pond Farm in Wilmot. The Seven to Save banner of the New Hampshire Preservation Alliance represents the group's successful efforts to preserve the property. *Melissa Crooker photograph.*

Award for Poetry. In 1995, she was named poet laureate of the state of New Hampshire. Much to the loss of New Hampshire and the world of poetry, she held that title just four months before her death at the age of forty-seven.

Donald Hall wrote elegantly and prolifically for much of his nearly ninety years. As writer of poetry, literary criticism, essays and children's books, he became one of the most recognizable authors of his time. For that output, he earned, among other honors, the Robert Frost Medal, the Ruth Lilly Poetry Prize, the James Laughlin Award and two Guggenheim Fellowships. From 1984 to 1989, he was the poet laureate of the state of New Hampshire. He was the 2006–07 United States poet laureate. Readers will find that Hall left behind a priceless legacy of writing to explain why he was so honored. On the prose side, I am especially partial to two of his books. *The Ox-Cart Man* (1979) tells for children of all ages a story of work and renewal, themes found in much of his work. I enjoy baseball and great essay writing, so my thanks go out to Donald Hall for combining them in 1985's *Fathers Playing Catch with Sons*. It's hard to say where to start with Donald Hall's poetry. Certainly, following their marriage, much of his work centered on his and

Jane Kenyon's life together. Sometimes blunt, always introspective, the work in which he deals with their life and her death might be a good start.

A subject that both poets addressed in their musings was their home at Eagle Pond Farm at 24 US Route 4 in Wilmot. Within sight of Mount Kearsarge, the rural, 160-acre site was where Donald Hall spent many summer days with his grandparents. The views, the settings and the trappings of everyday farm life were fodder for much of the couple's work and imagery. Now, thanks to the New Hampshire Preservation Alliance's Seven to Save program, Eagle Pond Farm will continue to inspire future generations. The farm that so nurtured its former residents will now offer public events as well as residencies for other writers.

For more information on Eagle Pond Farm, interested parties may write to At Eagle Pond, Inc., PO Box 452, Wilmot, New Hampshire, 03287 or email at.eagle.pond@gmail.com.

Chapter 14

ELIZABETH ORTON JONES AND CLARENCE WILLIAM ANDERSON

1910–2005 and 1891–1971
Mason

Elizabeth Orton Jones and C.W. Anderson, two friends, talented and beloved residents of Mason, are well remembered in town to this day. When Elizabeth Orton Jones moved to Mason in 1945, she was already well on her way to being recognized as one of the leading illustrators of children's books. During her time in Mason, she solidified that recognition. To her neighbors, she was known as Twig, a nickname derived from the title character of her 1942 book by the same name.

Just three years later, she was awarded the Caldecott Medal for her illustrations in Rachel Field's book *Prayers for a Child*. The medal is awarded each year by the American Library Association for the best illustrations in a children's book. A segment of Jones's comments on winning the award sum up nicely the philosophy she carried forward in her prolific career as an illustrator for the young. "Every child in the world has a hill, with a top to it. Every child—black, white, rich, poor, handicapped, unhandicapped. And singing is what the top of each hill is for."

Jones went on providing children with hills to sing from for the rest of her life, illustrating dozens of children's books. She also became an in integral part of her community in Mason. She edited *Mason Bicentennial, 1768–1968*.

C.W. Anderson, as he was known professionally, moved to Mason in the late 1930s and, like his friend Elizabeth Orton Jones, became a beloved and important part of the community. Anderson was best known for his Billy and Blaze books; these illustrated horse stories were renowned for their accuracy.

After moving to Mason, he taught art occasionally in the local schools and made use of local acquaintances and backgrounds in his stories. *Billy and Blaze: The Crooked Colt*, *The Lost Quarry* and *Blaze and the Gypsies* are a few of Anderson's books set against Mason backdrops.

BEYOND THE PAGE

In 1948, Elizabeth Orton Jones chose what is now Pickity Place restaurant, located at 248 Nutting Hill Road in Mason, as the model for her illustrations of Little Red Riding Hood (Little Golden Books). Visitors to Pickity Place today can dine and walk the grounds, rediscovering the charm Jones recognized on the property. Pickity Place is open 10:00 a.m. to 5:00 p.m. year-round. Dining is by telephone reservations only: 603-878-1151.

Andy's Summer Playhouse is located in Wilton Center and has provided opportunities for children to interact with professional artists. Andy's originated in Mason through

Top: Opened in 1974 as a restaurant, this cottage was used as a model by Elizabeth Orton Jones for her 1948 *Little Red Riding Hood*. *Gary Crooker photograph*.

Bottom: Located in historic Wilton Center, Andy's Summer Playhouse was named for noted writer and illustrator of children's books C.W. Anderson. *Gary Crooker photograph*.

the efforts of Margaret Sawyer and William Williams, two Mason teachers. It is named for C.W. Anderson and was heavily supported both artistically and financially for years by Anderson's friend and neighbor Elizabeth Orton Jones. Andy's usually presents two main-stage shows as well as a touring show and mini musicals. Telephone: 603-654-2613.

PART II

---◇◆◇---

BELKNAP, STRAFFORD AND ROCKINGHAM COUNTIES

Chapter 15

CELIA LAIGHTON THAXTER

1835–1894
Portsmouth

On his way to Maine in 1623, the English explorer Sir Christopher Levett dropped anchor at the Isle of Shoals. Among his brief notes pertaining to the rocky outcroppings about ten miles off the Maine/New Hampshire coast was the comment that "upon these islands I neither could see one good timber tree nor so much ground as to make a garden." He was right about the dearth of lumber, but as time and Celia Thaxter were to prove, he was off the mark about garden potential.

Celia Laighton first came to the Isle of Shoals in 1839 at the age of just four when her father, Thomas Laighton, took the job of lighthouse keeper on White Island. White is just one of nine islands that make up the storied archipelago. She was to spend the bulk of her fifty-nine years on those islands, and they were the most important influence on the impressive body of artistic work she produced. In addition to White, she also lived at different times on both Smuttynose and Appledore Islands. Remembered by many today as the poetess of the islands, she was also an artist and writer of prose who managed her accomplishments while coping with a family life that was anything but tranquil.

Her published writing began when the poem "Landlocked" appeared in the *Atlantic Monthly* magazine during a stretch of ten years living in Massachusetts with her husband and family. Even during that reluctant absence from her beloved Isles, the poem was inspired by them and expressed

Dedicated in 2014, the granite obelisk at Rye Harbor State Park commemorates Captain John Smith's mapping of the Isle of Shoals and Celia Thaxter's time there. *Melissa Crooker photograph.*

her frustration with being away. Nearly all her writing emerged from and spoke to her life away from the mainland.

Her most famous and anthologized poem is "The Sandpiper."

She also produced some high-quality prose. "A Memorable Murder" recounted the crime committed by sometimes Shoals resident and hired hand Louis Wagner. Appearing in the *Atlantic Monthly*, it is the story of one of New England's more lurid crimes of the nineteenth century. Wagner rowed the ten miles from the mainland and axe murdered two of the three defenseless women living there.

Much of Thaxter's writing income was necessary for paying household bills. Her husband, Levi Thaxter, had been her tutor as well as a business partner of her father. They married when she was just sixteen and he was thirty. Levi had fragile health and experienced a close brush with death when he was tossed from a boat during an island storm.

Those were both factors in the ten-year hiatus the couple had from the Shoals when they lived in Watertown and Newton, Massachusetts. Although they never officially divorced, they were separated for the most part once

Celia returned to Appledore with their three children. Their firstborn son, Karl, had mental and physical limitations that taxed her time and strength. In addition, she kept house, served as hostess at her father's busy hotel and kept a dedicated watch over the decline in health of her beloved, aging parents. In other words, much of her time was necessarily given over to her role as a caregiver.

Although much of her written work was done out of economic need, it delivered her into an elite literary circle that provided a creative outlet amid her busy days. The Appledore became a popular salon for many of the leading artists and writers of the day. Thomas Bailey Aldrich, Sarah Orne Jewett, John Greenleaf Whittier, Nathaniel Hawthorne and the impressionist artist Childe Hassam were just a few of the regular visitors to the island during Thaxter's time there.

Hassam became forever connected with another form of artwork that Celia Thaxter somehow managed to fit into her busy life. *An Island Garden*, her documentation of the creation and care of her front-yard garden, was illustrated by Hassam. For those who love gardens and the literature around them, it is a must read. In conjunction with the famous artist's pictures, Thaxter tells how she nurtured a bright and colorful garden in the most unlikely of settings. Her tales of daily battles with the birds (a friendly competition) and the slugs (a much fiercer confrontation) are a source of inspiration for gardeners everywhere.

It's not just gardeners and book lovers who are in Thaxter's debt. She also tried her hand at painting. Again combining a love of the artistic process with a continued need for income, the ever-resourceful Celia produced paintings on china and decorated many of her own poems with drawings. Her china pieces were much sought after in her day and are even more so now.

All these accomplishments should be viewed in the context of Thaxter's not inconsiderable responsibilities attached to the Isle of Shoals and her family. It was all achieved while seeing to her duties at the Appledore Hotel, mothering her children and dealing with a talented but mostly absent husband. She oversaw the decline and passing of her parents and, following their deaths, assumed the role of family leadership.

Might she have been an even more accomplished poetess if she was not shouldering all those other concerns? Probably. Although her garden, poetry, prose and artwork were all of a high quality, much of this work was done to pay the day-to-day bills, which just kept on coming.

Thaxter's life brings to mind Virginia Woolf's *A Room of One's Own*, which makes the point that over the ages, women were not allowed the type of

White Island Lighthouse,
Isles-of-Shoals, N. H.

Appledore Hotel, Isles of Shoals, N.H.

Top: White Island Lighthouse, where Thomas Laighton took the job of keeper. Laighton moved his entire family to the island with him, including his four-year-old daughter, Celia. *Postcard image.*

Bottom: Built in 1847 and burned in 1914, the Appledore Hotel was constructed by Thomas Laighton. For many years, his daughter Celia Thaxter served as hostess at the popular destination. *Postcard image.*

Opposite: Burned in the 1914 fire, Celia Thaxter's cottage was the site of her famous garden. The garden has been reconstructed and today is maintained by volunteers. *Postcard image.*

privacy and privilege that allowed their male counterparts the time to produce great literature. Woolf's famous creation, the theoretical poetess Judith Shakespeare, is the classic example. Was Celia Thaxter the sister of Shakespeare? No, but she was the daughter of Thomas and Eliza, the wife of Levi and the mother of Karl, John and Roland. And on top of all those duties to which she showed such a lifelong dedication, she was a terrific artist in various mediums who left us a wonderful garden of work to enjoy.

BEYOND THE PAGE

None of the footsteps of New Hampshire's literary lights are more enjoyable to follow than those of Celia Laighton Thaxter.

A good place to start following her trail might be at Rye Harbor State Park, located at 1730 Ocean Boulevard in Rye. The park is open year-round with metered parking and on clear days provides a view of the Isle of Shoals. Also on-site is the 1614 Monument, dedicated in 2014. The seventeen-foot, two-inch obelisk features four panels detailing Captain John Smith's exploration of the area as well as information on the Isle of Shoals and Celia Thaxter.

We took advantage of the Isle of Shoals Steamship Company's M/V *Thomas Laighton* for the Star Island Walking Tour and Portsmouth Harbor Tour. Although the day of our excursion was wet and foggy, the trip was well worth it. The approximately three-hour round trip is superbly narrated both ways. The ship docks at Star Island for about one hour, which provides ample time for an informative walking tour. Prices are reasonable, with senior citizen discounts available. Contact number: 603-431-5500.

Also available is a day trip to Appledore Island via the University of New Hampshire Research Vessel R/V *Gulf Challenger*. Cruise space is limited to a first-come-first-serve basis, and travelers should be capable of several miles of walking. Fees are $50 for adults and $40 per child. The tour includes a visit to the recreated gardens of Celia Thaxter. Contact: shoals.lab@unh.edu.

Chapter 16

THOMAS BAILEY ALDRICH

1836–1907
Portsmouth

So, you know Tom Sawyer and his partner in mischief, right? Tom and Huckleberry Finn are familiar names to even the most casual followers of the American literary scene. But did you know that at least some of the seeds that grew into these two icons of boyhood were planted right here on New Hampshire's seacoast? But we'll circle back to that.

First, let's meet Portsmouth's own Thomas Bailey Aldrich. He was born in Portsmouth in 1836, but his parents moved away when he was just three years old. He returned from 1849 to 1852 to live with his maternal grandfather, Thomas D. Bailey. There can be no better place and time for a young man to be than Portsmouth in the summer. Aldrich made the best of it, using those formative years as the basis for his most famous work, *The Story of a Bad Boy*.

The Story of a Bad Boy is a semi-autobiographical set of tales recognized as one of the earliest realistic treatments of American childhood. The book itself is a compilation of the adventures of Bailey and his youthful cohorts in Portsmouth. The city itself is thinly veiled as "Rivermouth," and the author is equally recognizable as the narrator, "Tom Bailey."

There is some truth to the old saying that you can't tell a book by its cover. However, you can tell a tale by its truthfulness. That is the reason *The Story of a Bad Boy* is deservedly described as the first realistic book in a long line of "bad boy" stories. Chapter titles often fail to live up to their promise, but here, they deliver, with the true-to-form type of youthful escapades that readers appreciate. "On Board the Typhoon," "The Adventures of the Fourth," "The Snow Fort on Slatter's Hill" and "How We Astonished the Rivermouthians" are all good examples. The "Cruise of the Dolphin" chapter is a tragic but realistic bit of writing that sold me on the author's ability to put away his rose-colored glasses when reflecting on childhood.

Although *The Story of a Bad Boy* remains by far the most remembered of Aldrich's books, there was much more to his portfolio. While working in his uncle's business in New York, Aldrich contributed to many area magazines and newspapers. He also became acquainted and sometimes friends with other local writers such as Walt Whitman and Bayard Taylor. During the Civil War, he served as editor of the *New York Illustrated News*. Following the war, Aldrich's continued work in an editorial role became an important part of his legacy. From 1866 to 1874, he edited the Boston-based magazine *Every Saturday*. As editor for the life of the magazine, he published works by many of the leading lights of the day, including Wilkie Collins, Charles Dickens, Thomas Hardy and Alfred Tennyson.

Aldrich's best-remembered wielding of the editorial pencil came during the years 1881 to 1890, when he was directing the fortunes of the *Atlantic*. It was a tumultuous nine years as he frequently clashed with his publisher, but his successes were many, and the magazine flourished under his guidance. He attracted top writers to its pages. Perhaps none of the pieces he published were more important than the short stories of African American writer Charles Chesnutt. "The Goophered Grapevine" and "Po Sandy" appeared first in the *Atlantic* and were the lead stories in Chesnutt's *The Conjure Woman*, which appeared in book form in 1899. The very light-skinned Chesnutt could have easily passed as white but chose not to. Instead, he used his writing to address such uncomfortable subjects as miscegenation, lynching and the hypocrisy of Jim Crow.

Aldrich's role providing a platform for other writers didn't preclude a prolific career of his own as both a poet and writer of fiction. Like *The Story of a Bad Boy*, many of his books drew heavily on his time in Portsmouth. Readers will recognize his boyhood town in books like *A Rivermouth Romance* (1877) and *An Old Town by the Sea* (1883).

Thomas Bailey Aldrich has been quoted as saying, "A man is known by the company his mind keeps." By that standard, his mind certainly ran in elite circles. Among his close associates and friends in the literary world, he numbered Henry Longfellow, Henry James and Walt Whitman. But perhaps his closest confidant was Samuel L. Clemens, who, of course, wrote as Mark Twain. The meeting of the two in 1871 was the beginning of a close thirty-six-year friendship. To circle back to our original mention of

The dining room of Thomas Bailey Aldrich's home, where he entertained many famous authors of the day, including his friend Mark Twain. *Postcard image.*

Thomas Bailey Aldrich lived here from 1849 to 1852 and gathered many of the youthful experiences relayed in *Diary of a Bad Boy*. Aldrich later lived here as an adult, and the house is now part of Strawbery Banke. *Postcard image.*

Tom and Huck's connection with Aldrich, *The Story of a Bad Boy* appeared in 1870. Tom Bailey and his young "Rivermouthians" were quite likely precursors to Twain's duo. *The Adventures of Tom Sawyer* appeared in 1876. Compare the two Toms and insert Portsmouth for Hannibal, Missouri, and the connections are plain to see.

BEYOND THE PAGE

The house of Aldrich's grandfather Thomas Bailey is now a part of Strawbery Banke Museum in Portsmouth. Adjacent to the house is the Thomas Bailey Aldrich Memorial Garden. The house is open for tours during regular museum hours. Strawbery Banke is open twelve months out of the year. For specific hours, fees and events, contact info@sbmuseum.org or 603-453-1100.

Just down the street from Strawbery Banke at 371 Court Street is Aldrich Park. Take a break and relax in the same area where Aldrich and his youthful pals played.

Chapter 17

HELEN DORE BOYLSTON

1895–1984
Portsmouth

One of the most important things to know about Helen Dore Boylston and her writing is that she was the real deal. Let me explain.

When I first entered the antiquarian book world in the 1970s, it was pretty much as a picker for dealers who actually knew what they were doing. It was a trial-and-error education if ever there was one. At the time, one type of book that was highly sought after was children's series books. The Hardy Boys, Nancy Drew, the Bobbsey Twins and Tom Swift, particularly in their original dust jackets, were sure sales for my itinerant side hustle. Those searches are how I became acquainted with the Sue Barton book series by New Hampshire's own Helen Dore Boylston.

Boylston came by her qualifications to write *Sue Barton, Student Nurse* through her own experiences. Born in Portsmouth in 1895 to a dentist father and schoolteacher mother, she was educated in local schools. Her youthful nickname Troub, short for trouble, might have given a clue to the adventurous life that lay ahead. A year at Simmons College was followed by graduation as a nurse from Massachusetts General Hospital in 1915. It was the right start for someone who would go on to produce a seven-book series based on nursing. But her adventurous life was just getting underway.

Boylston served in World War I as part of the British Expeditionary Force as a nurse anesthetist. She reached the rank of captain during the war and wrote about her time at the front in her 1927 book *Sister: The War Diary of a Nurse*.

Three of the titles from the seven-book Sue Barton series of children's books written by New Hampshire native Helen Dore Boylston. *Gary Crooker photograph.*

The adventure bug was by no means done with her yet. Staying in Europe, she applied her nursing skills on the Continent for the Red Cross. A chance meeting on a train trip while there resulted in a lifelong friendship and another push in the direction of writing for a living. Her newfound friend was Rose Wilder Lane, who was working as a reporter. Lane was the daughter of Laura Ingalls Wilder, who would later become famous for the Little House on the Prairie series of children's books.

Boylston continued to add experiences that would eventually find their way into print. In 1926, she and new friend Rose Lane traveled from Paris to Albania in a Model T Ford at a time when auto travel was still quite adventurous. Her account of that trip, culled from letters and journals, was published in 1983 as *Travels with Zenobia: Paris to Albania by Model T Ford.*

The relationship between the two writers continued as they returned to the United States, living on the property of Laura Ingalls Wilder. But when the 1929 depression saw Boylston lose significant investments, they went their separate ways. Boylston returned to New Hampshire, and her career as a full-time writer flourished. Many articles under her byline started appearing in prominent magazines of the day, and in 1936, the Sue Barton phase of her writing journey got started.

The variety of her nursing experience worked its way realistically into the character and adventures of Sue Barton. *Sue Barton, Student Nurse* was published in 1936, marking the successful start to a seven-volume series. *Sue Barton, Senior Nurse* (1937); *Sue Barton, Visiting Nurse* (1938); *Sue Barton, Rural Nurse* (1939); *Sue Barton, Superintendent Nurse* (1940); *Sue Barton, Neighborhood*

Nurse (1949); and *Sue Barton, Staff Nurse* (1952) all touched on aspects of Boylston's firsthand experience in the nursing field.

Even her four-book series about a young actress named Carol, while not derived from actual acting experience, was authoritative nonetheless, as she drew on the experiences of her friend and neighbor Eva Le Gallienne. Le Gallienne was a successful Broadway actress and founder of the Civic Repertory Theater. That collaboration resulted in *Carol Goes Backstage* (1941), *Carol Plays Summer Stock* (1942), *Carol Goes on Stage* (1943) and *Carol on Tour* (1946).

So, in the vast sea of series books that dominated children's literature in the first half of the twentieth century, what made Helen Dore Boylston stand out as the real thing? What set her byline apart from Franklin Dixon's Hardy Boys series or Carolyn Keene's Nancy Drew books or Victor Appleton and his Tom Swift tales? Those were all series that admirably introduced generations of young people to the world of reading. The difference is that none of the authors were real at all. Dixon, Keene and Appleton were house pseudonyms of the Stratemeyer Syndicate publishing company. Sue Barton was the creation of the very real Helen Dore Boylston of Portsmouth, New Hampshire.

Chapter 18

GRACE METALIOUS

1924–1964
Gilmanton

Every generation has their cultural touchstones that helped shape their view of the world they lived in. My parents' contemporaries had Pearl Harbor and D-Day, while mine had the Kennedy assassination. From a literary point of view, I personally add another. I remember when *Peyton Place* by Grace Metalious was considered a dirty book.

The blockbuster novel was inspired by real-life events in the town of Gilmanton, where Metalious spent ten hours a day composing what was to become a publishing phenomenon. When the book was finally picked up by the small publishing house of Julian Messner, its success was immediate and unprecedented. On publication in 1956, sales soared. *Peyton Place*, initially titled *The Tree and the Blossom*, was on the New York Times bestseller list a week before it was released and sold one hundred thousand copies in the first month. It remained on the list for fifty-nine consecutive weeks.

Although such sales were unheard of for a first novel, Grace Metalious was no overnight success. Born Marie Grace DeRepentigny, she grew up in Manchester in a poor and broken home. The only real constant in her young life seemed to be her dream to be a writer. Always a voracious reader, she read and wrote poetry throughout her days at Manchester Central High School.

On graduation, she married George Metalious, a high school sweetheart. George joined the army, served in France, had an affair. They had three children together, moved to Belmont and then to Gilmanton. George, who had acquired a degree from the University of New Hampshire under the GI Bill, took teaching jobs in both towns. While Grace harvested scandal from the communities past and present, many townsfolk reciprocated by whispering tales, some true, of her bad parenting and housekeeping. But through it all, she kept writing.

Many citizens of Gilmanton were famously unhappy with both Grace and her book. Most reviews of the book and its unusually frank dealings with small-town scandal were negative. The book was banned in several communities because of its treatment of taboo subjects such as rape, suicide and incest. Everyone seemed to abhor *Peyton Place* except the reading public. With money advanced for the promise of two more novels, Grace purchased what she described as her dream house on 528 Meadow Pond Road in Gilmanton.

Success continued beyond the printed page as Hollywood jumped on the wagon. Although Grace was unhappy with the sanitized 1957 movie version of *Peyton Place*, it was a success at the box office. The film boosted Grace's bank account and received nine Academy Award nominations. Later movie adaptations of Peyton Place were less successful. She followed up her blockbuster with three moderately successful novels: *Return to Peyton Place* (1959), *The Tight White Collar* (1961) and the heavily autobiographical *No Adam in Eden* (1963). They did sell well but not in the range of her original success.

The realization of a life as a successful author didn't translate into happiness in other areas of Grace's life. She and George divorced and then remarried two years later. In between, a two-year marriage to T.J. Martin also failed. Several other unwise and unhappy relationships mixed with a life of heavy drinking led to health and financial problems Grace couldn't overcome.

Peyton Place repeated its success on television's small screen in 1964 as it grabbed blockbuster status once more. It began a five-year run as the original prime-time soap opera as well as launching the acting careers of Mia Farrow and Ryan O'Neal.

But this was success that Grace was never able to witness. Seven months prior to the show's premiere, Grace Metalious passed away from liver disease in Boston's Beth Israel Hospital. It was discovered after her death that she was financially insolvent.

Like many before her, Grace Metalious ended her life consumed by the very success and fame she had spent so much time and effort pursuing. She

Currently the Gilmanton Winery and Restaurant at 528 Meadow Pond Road; formerly the site of Grace Metalious's dream home. *Melissa Crooker photograph.*

once said she would prefer to be poor if she could live her life over: "Before I was successful I was as happy as anyone gets."

In retrospect, what offended critics the most seemed to be not how well she presented her subject matter—it was that she presented the subject matter at all. To say the least, 1950s America was squeamish about the subjects of rape, sex and incest. The uproar, of course, was paired with readers purchasing the offending book at a record pace.

Peyton Place is not Shakespeare, and I've never read a review that claimed it was. But it is a pretty well-written story. It indeed deals with subjects that make many readers uncomfortable even today. But it also presents the women within its pages as real people with real hopes and dreams for their own lives. In other words, it was a mid-1950s novel with some feminist themes ahead of their time.

BEYOND THE PAGE

For more information on the youth of Grace Metalious, I would highly recommend the work of Manchester native and author Robert B. Perreault. His book *Franco-American Life and Culture in Manchester New Hampshire* contains an informed chapter dedicated to Grace's upbringing and experiences in the city. In the chapter "Before Peyton Place," Perreault identifies many of the city locations important to Grace's early life.

Grace Metalious wasted no time in investing her newfound wealth. On the signing of her second book contract, she purchased the aforementioned property at 528 Meadow Pond Road. The house and grounds are now the site of the Gilmanton Winery and Restaurant. The owners have not only accepted the legacy of the famous former owner—they have embraced it. A small display near the front of the restaurant includes a stack of Metalious books and a picture of her at work. The restaurant is open 11:00 a.m. to 6:00 p.m. on Thursday, Friday and Saturday. On Sunday, the hours are 8:30 a.m. to 5:00 p.m. Reservations are suggested by calling 603-267-8251. My wife and I can attest to the appeal of both the prices and the French toast.

The grave site of Grace Metalious is located in the Smith Meeting House Cemetery on Meeting House Road in Gilmanton. A marble gravestone states quite simply, "Grace Metalious (1924–1964)." Stubbornly independent to the end, Grace chose Gilmanton as her final resting place, much to the chagrin of many of the town's residents. While the stone marker might suggest a short, uneventful life, it in fact marks the end of a woman who was ahead of her time in many ways. Her life was short but certainly anything but uneventful.

Chapter 19

ROBERT FROST

1874–1963

Derry

While I've tried to arrange the subjects of this book somewhat by geography, poet Robert Frost is an example of the difficulties that can arise in a small state like New Hampshire. First, we have to establish the fact that Frost belongs in the panoply of New Hampshire writers to begin with. Then there is the problem of which part of the state we actually place him in.

Many places in the United States and even the world can lay at least partial claim to the four-time Pulitzer Prize–winning poet. Born in San Francisco in 1874, he moved to Lawrence, Massachusetts, in 1885 with his widowed mother. Lawrence could certainly stake a claim in the Frost competition, as he not only graduated from Lawrence High but also eventually married his co-valedictorian, Elinor White. Frost spent 1921, 1925 and 1926 at the University of Michigan. He was named poet laureate of neighboring Vermont by an act of that state's legislature. He lived in England from 1912 to 1915, where he published his first book of poetry, *A Boy's Will*, in 1913.

Obviously, many different areas can lay claim to the man Robert Frost. But the poet Robert Frost was definitely of New England and specifically New Hampshire. The rural themes in so much of his poetry exude the New Hampshire years—and no wonder. He attended college at Dartmouth for two years. In 1896, he and Elinor honeymooned in Allenstown. From 1900 to 1911, he and his growing family worked a farm in Derry while he taught English at nearby Pinkerton Academy. The years 1915 to 1920 saw

A youthful Robert Frost on his way to becoming one of America and the world's most beloved poets. *Postcard image.*

Frost and his family move to Franconia and again take up the farming life. For our purposes, we will locate Frost in Derry, where his rural sensibilities were nurtured for eleven years.

Now that we have placed Robert Frost geographically in the context of this book, let me relate my introduction to the poet. In 1961, I was in my eleventh year, and while I was already a voracious reader, I can't say I was a big fan of poetry. "Casey at the Bat" and "Take Me Out to the Ballgame" seemed like rhymes enough for me—those and a few of the ribald limericks that were staples of the elementary recess scene. My reading tended more toward heroes of the athletic or military type, like so many other eleven-year-olds.

That being said, I did know who Robert Frost was. That's another of the benefits of a reading life, even at an early age. You might think you are just getting enjoyment from stories of adventure, when in fact names like Frost and snippets of his poetry are sneaking in.

So, in 1961, when I heard that the newly elected president, John F. Kennedy, was going to have Robert Frost read a poem at his inauguration, it struck a chord. Politics and all of that "real world stuff" actually had a place for people who wrote poems and stories? Eureka! I remember, as many my age probably do, that there was lots of snow during the week preceding the ceremonies. It was sunny the day of the inauguration, but the combination of the glare and his aging eyes made it impossible for the eighty-six-year-old Frost to read his prepared poem. Instead, he recited from memory "The Gift," a poem he had composed back in 1942. Not a bad improvisation for an octogenarian before a national audience.

Derry, Franconia, Hanover and Allenstown: Frost certainly spread himself all over the Granite State at different times in his life. In turn, New Hampshire is spread throughout his poetry. His very first Pulitzer came in 1924 and was awarded for his 1923 volume of poetry *New Hampshire*. In it are many of what came to be his most popular poems, including "Fire and Ice," "Stopping by Woods on a Snowy Evening" and "Nothing Gold Can

Stay." *Collected Poems* (1931), *A Further Range* (1937) and *A Witness Tree* (1943) all continued the Pulitzer run that made Frost the sole four-time winner in the poetry category.

While Frost's poetry certainly belongs to the world, he will forever be associated with his New Hampshire years.

BEYOND THE PAGE

The farm in Derry where Robert and Elinor Frost lived and worked with their growing family from 1900 to 1911 is maintained as the Robert Frost Farm State Historic Site. It is located at 122 Rockingham Road. The park and farmhouse are open daily from 10:00 a.m. to 4:00 p.m. with tours on the hour ending at 3:00 p.m. The trails and grounds are open from dusk until dawn year-round. For up-to-date fees, hours and restrictions, check the New Hampshire State Parks website.

The Frost Place in Franconia is a self-described "permanent home and museum for poets and poetry." Now owned by the Town of Franconia, the former home of Frost from 1915 to 1920 is located at 158 Ridge Road. Contact for hours and events: 603-823-5510 or frost@frostplace.org.

New Hampshire Historical Marker No. 230, commemorating Robert and Elinor Frost's time in Allenstown on their honeymoon in a cottage near the Suncook River. *Melissa Crooker photograph.*

Robert Frost's time in New Hampshire is the subject of two of the state's historical roadside markers. State marker No. 126 is located at the site of the Derry farm and reads:

> *Robert Frost 1874–1963. Some of the best-loved poems in the English language are associated with this small farm owned by the poet from 1900 to 1911. Here Frost farmed, taught at nearby Pinkerton Academy and developed the poetic voice which later won him the Pulitzer Prize for poetry four times and world fame as one of our foremost poets.*

State marker No. 230 in Allenstown deals with an earlier but also significant interlude in Frost's life.

> *In the summer of 1896, aspiring poet Robert Frost (1874–1963) and his wife Elinor spent a belated honeymoon in a rented cottage near the Suncook River in Allenstown. Carl Burell, a high school friend and avid naturalist, was foreman at the Moulton box shop at Buck Street dam. Botany walks with Burell awakened Frost to the natural world, coloring his later writings. Frost recalled these walks in "The Quest of the Orchis" (1901). Burell's 1896 injury in a mill accident inspired Frost's poem, "The Self-Seeker."*

Chapter 20

SAM WALTER FOSS

1858–1911
Candia

Bring me men to match my mountains, / Bring me men to match my plains." Those stirring lines originated from the pen of Sam Walter Foss of Candia in one of his most famous poems. The lines are probably more familiar to most people than the poet.

Sam Walter Foss was born in Candia and educated locally before going off to Brown University. Such was his career at the Ivy League school that his name appears on the prestigious Brown Mace. Other distinguished alumni so honored include Samuel Gridley Howe, John Hay and Charles Evans Hughes.

Foss went on to a long and distinguished career as librarian at the Somerville, Massachusetts public library. He also turned out five volumes of poetry, much of it of the "down home" variety and not much remembered today—except for the lines above from his poem "The Coming American" and one other poem called "The House by the Side of the Road."

The lines from "The Coming American" cited above were, until 2003, inscribed on the wall at the United States Air Force Academy. Today, they can be found inscribed at Epcot Center in Florida. The second poem contains the line "Let me live in a house by the side of the road and be a friend to man." Because baseball and literature always seem to be connected for me, my first exposure to the lines were Detroit Tigers announcer Ernie Harwell's catchphrase after a strikeout: "He stood there like the house by the side of the road and watched that one go by."

Located, appropriately enough, by the side of the road is New Hampshire Historical Marker No. 141 detailing the career of Candia's Sam Walter Foss. *Melissa Crooker photograph.*

BEYOND THE PAGE

New Hampshire Historical Marker No. 141 is in Candia at the junction of NH 43 and Business Route 101.

Candia is the birthplace of the well-known poet, journalist and publisher, Sam Walter Foss. Son of Dyer and Polly Foss, he was born June 19, 1858. His homespun verse and country poems were great favorites.

"The House by the Side of the Road," the most popular, was believed to have been inspired by his boyhood home, on Brown Road, in this town.

PART III

---◇◆◇---

COOS, GRAFTON AND CARROLL COUNTIES

Chapter 21

ELEANOR EMILY
HODGMAN PORTER

1868–1920
Littleton

W e used to have a little camp in Lunenberg, Vermont. It's a small border town just a twenty-five-minute drive to Littleton, New Hampshire. At least once a year, we would set aside a full day to make the trek and spend hours walking what we have always felt is one of the finest main streets in all of New England. We were always glad to be there. After all, it is New Hampshire's "Glad Town."

In parts of Littleton, it is always 1913 and a young lady named Pollyanna Whittier is always giving residents and visitors reasons to be glad. Thanks to native author Eleanor H. Porter, that should continue to be the case for many years to come.

There seemed to be every bit as much sad as glad in the childhood of author Porter. But those experiences provided much of the basis for *Pollyanna*, her most popular and well-known novel. Born Eleanor Emily Hodgman at the home of her maternal grandparents in December 1868, her early life didn't seem to bode well for a career as a successful author. But a closer look reveals a childhood that contained many of the seeds for later bestselling stories.

While she was a schoolgirl in Littleton, Eleanor's parents divorced, not that common an occurrence in Victorian-era New England. A year later, in 1876, her father died. Eleanor's mother was a sickly woman most of her adult life, and Eleanor herself struggled with fragile health. Her health became so bad she was withdrawn from the Littleton school system and tutored privately at home. To aid her daughter through those difficult times, her mother devised a game that involved seeking out silver linings to problems. The object of the game was to find something good in even the worst of circumstances. It was a theme that would recur throughout her writings, particularly in her most popular novel.

Despite receiving that literary inspiration early in her life, Eleanor's ambitions and talents pointed in another direction at the beginning of her adult life. After the end of her homeschooling, she applied and was accepted to study at the New England Conservatory for Music. Always noted for her singing voice, she studied in Boston and continued her career as a singer until her marriage to Lyman Porter of Corinth, Vermont.

At the time of her marriage, Eleanor was still fifteen years away from becoming a serious full-time novelist. Success came early in her pursuit, though, as her first novel sold very well. She published her first full-length book, *Cross Currents*, in 1908, at the age of thirty-nine. It is the story of Margaret, a young girl on her own whose attitude and resilience affect everyone she meets. It enjoyed solid sales and was prescient of the winning formula that would make one of her characters a household name and, eventually, a dictionary-worthy word.

Cross Currents was followed in rapid succession by *The Turn of the Tide* (1908), *The Story of Marco* (1911), *Miss Billy* (1911) and *Miss Billy's Decision* (1912). Then came *Pollyanna* in 1913, and Eleanor Hodgman Porter became one of the most popular authors of her generation. The story of young Pollyanna Whittier tells of one girl's mission to cheer up an entire town. Arriving orphaned in fictional Beldingsville, Vermont, Pollyanna proceeds to instruct her grumpy new neighbors in the ways of the "glad" game taught to her by her minister father. By simply instructing those around her to look on the sunny side of whatever life brings, she transforms her melancholy fellow citizens through her optimism.

Simplistic? Sure, but that simple recipe proved to be just what America was looking for. The book became a runaway bestseller. Parker Brothers produced a Pollyanna board game, and that, too, flew off the shelves. Restaurants, boardinghouses and mountain cabins all took on the name of Porter's creation. Glad Clubs sprang up all over the country in honor of Pollyanna's philosophy.

The stage and screen treatment soon followed the success of the book. Helen Hayes depicted Pollyanna on Broadway in 1916. In 1920, war-weary Americans swarmed to motion picture theaters to watch one of America's

Unveiled in 2002, this statue of Eleanor Porter's Pollyanna graces the Littleton Library lawn and has served as the center of the Glad Day celebrations. *Elizabeth Crooker photograph.*

sweethearts, Pollyanna, played by another, Mary Pickford. In 1960, the irrepressibly optimistic icon received the inevitable Disney treatment with the release of a film with Hayley Mills in the lead.

Of course, every action creates a reaction. Porter's success was greeted with disdain by many critics. They dismissed her work as overly sentimental and not based in reality. Eleanor Porter, who knew a few things about hard

Above: The Pollyanna display at the Littleton Historical Society showing the many facets of popular culture affected by Eleanor Porter's character. *Melissa Crooker photograph.*

Left: Pollyanna fans and visitors are greeted with this sign entering Littleton's Main Street in early June each year. *Melissa Crooker photograph.*

COOS, GRAFTON AND CARROLL COUNTIES

reality herself, countered her critics with a reply sounding much like her own Pollyanna: "I have never believed that we ought to deny discomfort and pain and evil; I have merely thought that it is far better to greet the unknown with a cheer." She certainly had the last laugh. *Pollyanna* stayed on the bestseller list for three years, hitting eighth place in 1913, second in 1914 and fourth in 1915. Her equally optimistic tale *Just David* earned a spot on the bestseller list in 1915.

Merriam-Webster defines a "Pollyanna" as "a person characterized by irrepressible optimism and a tendency to find good in everything." Sounds like pretty good traits in a person, but the term is most often used in a pejorative sense by the more cynical among us. Both Eleanor and Pollyanna would have seen the bright side of even those sentiments.

In her relatively short career, Eleanor Hodgman Porter left a legacy of bestselling novels and optimistic attitudes that live on. The engraving on the base of her hometown's Pollyanna statue sums it up well. "Author Eleanor Hodgman Porter (1868–1920), was born and lived in Littleton, New Hampshire. In 1913 she created the cheerful Pollyanna, the world famous character, whose very name inspires an understanding of gladness and optimism."

It was good that Eleanor led such a fruitful and productive life, because her early health problems stayed with her, and she passed away in 1920 at the age of fifty-one.

BEYOND THE PAGE

In June 2002, the now familiar bronze statue of Pollyanna was unveiled on the lawn of the Littleton library. Commissioned by the Eames family of Littleton and created by New Hampshire artist Emile Birch, the sculpture serves as the focal point for Pollyanna Glad Days every second Saturday in June. In 2019, Governor Chris Sununu signed a bill designating that date statewide as Pollyanna of Littleton Recognition Day.

When in town, also be sure to visit the Littleton Area Historical Society. It is located in the historic Littleton Opera House and includes a small but highly informative display of Eleanor Porter/Pollyanna memorabilia. The society rooms are located on 4 Rogers Street and are open 10:00 a.m. to 3:00 p.m. on Wednesday and Saturday. An appropriately cheerful and helpful staff will go out of their way to handle any questions.

On 91 Main Street, a visit to the GoLittleton Glad Shop offers Pollyanna-themed souvenirs, Littleton mementos and Glad Gifts. Started in 2019 by organizer Veronica Francis, the shop is open from 10:00 a.m. to 2:00 p.m. on Sundays, 11:00 a.m. to 2:00 p.m. on Saturdays and 11:00 a.m. to 4:00 p.m. on weekdays.

Chapter 22

ERNEST COOK POOLE

1880–1950
Franconia

During his later years, in what was then the Sugar Hill section of Franconia, Ernest Poole was a walking companion of Robert Frost. He also wrote a popular, and quite insightful, book on local folks and folklore called *The Great White Hills of New Hampshire*. As bucolic and laid-back an existence as that may sound, it belies a youthful writing career that saw Poole muckraking inner-city life, visiting Russia and admiring many results of the 1917 revolution and eventually joining the Socialist Party of America.

Following graduation from Princeton, Poole moved into University Settlement House in New York. This was the beginning of a career observing and writing about many of the seedier sides of American life from a definite left-leaning point of view. He continued to live in and write about the plight of New York's inner-city residents for several years.

It was in 1915 that Poole brought out the first of his novels highlighting his beliefs. *The Harbor* treated trade unions sympathetically, one of the first to do so. While this first novel was greeted enthusiastically by many critics and readers, it was his next effort that won him the most acclaim. *His Family*, published in 1917, tells a story with settings moving back and forth between New Hampshire and the inner city. Poole drew on his tenement house experiences once again. The result was a book that was honored with the very first Pulitzer Prize in the novel category in 1918. Now known as the Pulitzer Prize for Fiction, it was first of its kind awarded. Although he is not a household name today, Ernest Poole's writings were highly influential in their day. First editions of *His Family* are highly sought after by collectors because of the novel's status as receiver of the first Pulitzer for fiction awarded.

Poole was sent to Russia by the *Saturday Evening Post* to observe the Russian Revolution. His sympathetic observations resulted in a pair of nonfiction works. *The Dark People: Russia's Crisis* and *The Village: Russian Impressions* both came out of his reporting experiences in 1918.

Chapter 23

THEODOR SEUSS GEISEL

1904–1995
Hanover

Theodor Seuss Geisel was born in Springfield, Massachusetts. Of that there is no doubt. On March 2, 1904, in the town he later turned to for the title of his very first children's book. But a case can certainly be made that his more famous pen name, Dr. Seuss, was born in Hanover, New Hampshire, during his undergraduate days at Dartmouth College.

Of course, there were signs of what might come even in his days at Central High in Springfield. At the tender age of fourteen he penned a pretty witty parody of Walt Whitman's "O Captain! My Captain!" under the title "O Latin." He regularly contributed to the school's newspaper and held the title of boys' news editor. In his senior yearbook, classmates named him both Class Artist and Class Wit—certainly more prescient than the average high school yearbook prediction.

Partially out of admiration for a beloved English teacher at Central High School who had been a Dartmouth graduate, Theodor Geisel joined the class of 1925 at the New Hampshire Ivy League school. In 1921, when he entered college, Theodore Geisel's family's fortunes took a turn for the worse as the Volstead Act and Prohibition closed down the family brewery. It wouldn't be the last time Prohibition affected Geisel's fortunes.

Once at Dartmouth, Geisel threw himself into the same interests he had in high school. He immediately became a contributor to the school's humor magazine, the *Jack-O-Lantern*. He also submitted items for the school's paper,

Theodor Geisel, a.k.a. Dr. Seuss, created nearly seventy books under the Seuss pseudonym, which he first used during his time at Dartmouth. *Library of Congress.*

the *Daily Dartmouth.* It was in his junior year that he discovered what he called the "excitement" of marrying words and pictures: "I began thinking that words and pictures, married, might possibly produce a progeny more interesting than either parent."

But it was Prohibition, and the fact that college students were bound to ignore it, that first brought the Seuss byline into being. In his senior year, Geisel was caught sharing a bottle of gin with fellow students and called before the dean. The result was a suspension from all extracurricular activities for the remainder of the year. That, of course, included any contributions to school publications by Theodor Geisel—but not by Seuss. In the April edition of the *Jack-O-Lantern,* a couple of cartoons appeared signed by "Seuss" and "T. Seuss." Seuss, his mother's maiden name and his middle, made its debut as his identifying signature as the result of a youthful indiscretion at school.

Of course, Dr. Seuss still had lots of places to go and things to see once his time in Dartmouth and New Hampshire was done. Over sixty books appeared over his lifetime with the byline Dr. Seuss. When he only wrote the book but didn't do the illustrations, his pseudonym would change to Theo LeSieg, simply making use of his name spelled backwards.

Geisel studied for a time at Oxford before leaving school behind and worked as an illustrator for both magazines and advertising campaigns. His work for Standard Oil created one of the most popular ad slogans of the pre–World War II era. Promoting the company's mosquito insecticide with words and cartoons, Geisel made the words "Quick, Henry! The Flit" one of the longest-running catchphrases in advertising.

In 1943, Dr. Seuss gave way as Theodor Geisel joined the war effort. Put in charge of the animation department of the Motion Picture Unit, he emerged in 1946 with the rank of lieutenant colonel. He stayed in the movie business for a while following the war but soon started churning out the string of popular children's books that would make him a household name—or at least a household pseudonym.

The man Random House editor Bennett Cerf called the only true genius he ever had in his years at the publishing house became the biggest name in the business. But through all the fame and fortune that followed him, his days at Dartmouth remained an influence on his writing. Two out of the last three books he ever published came with nods to his alma mater.

You're Only Old Once: A Book for Obsolete Children (1986) begins with the following dedication to his former New Hampshire classmates: "With Affection for and Affliction with the Members of the Class of 1925." Just as sales for *How the Grinch Stole Christmas* explode each Christmas, another Geisel title has become a perennial bestseller come June and graduation time. Seuss himself told the story of the verbal handshake that was shared when Dartmouth students met. "Oh the places you'll go!" was answered with "The people you'll meet!"—certainly explaining the title of 1990's *Oh the Places You'll Go!*

Beyond the Page

In 2012, Dartmouth named its medical school, the fourth oldest in the nation, the Audrey and Theodor Geisel School of Medicine after the author and his wife. In dedication remarks at the time, Dartmouth president Jim Yong Kim noted it was a tribute to "two individuals whose work continues to change the world for the better."

For students looking to immerse themselves in the Seussian world, there is the Theodor Seuss Geisel Room in Baker Library at Dartmouth. In addition to a bronze bas relief of Seuss characters, there is a portrait of Seuss. Display cases with memorabilia and figures from the world of Seuss complete the room.

Chapter 24

EDWARD ESTLIN CUMMINGS

1894–1962

Madison

Place can certainly be a factor for those in the creative arts. For Edward Estlin Cummings, a giant among twentieth-century poets, one of those places, both as a child and as an adult, was the Joy Farm on Silver Lake in Madison, New Hampshire.

Cummings first started coming to the idyllic setting when he was just five years old, in 1899. That was when his parents purchased the property from local farmer Ephraim Joy. From that time forward, Cummings spent at least part of his summers there for the rest of his life when in the United States.

Of course, despite the New Hampshire influence, there was much more to Cummings's life and art. In 1917, Cummings joined the Norton-Harjes Ambulance Corps for service in World War I and headed for Europe. Cummings and fellow writer William Slater Brown met while crossing the Atlantic for duty. Their service was cut short when some of their letters home containing anti-war sentiments caught the attention of French authorities. Imprisonment for over three months in France became the basis for Cummings 1922 novel *The Enormous Room*. The highly praised novel features much of the unconventional grammar for which Cummings is remembered. Despite the fact that Cummings would go on to be highly acclaimed as a poet, his autobiographical novel was praised by F. Scott Fitzgerald, who said, "Of all work by young men who have sprung up since 1920 one book survives—The Enormous Room by e e cummings."

Above: Mount Chocorua, which served as inspiration for E.E. Cummings and many other writers and artists through the years. *Postcard image.*

Right: Poet and artist Edward Estlin Cummings, who spent many of his youthful and adult summers at Joy Farm in Madison. *Library of Congress.*

Following his return to America, Joy Farm continued to be a summer retreat for Cummings his entire life, although it held some unhappy memories for him. When he was a child, his beloved dog Rex drowned when a canoeing trip went bad. In 1926, his father was killed en route to Joy Farm when his automobile was struck by an oncoming train in Center Ossipee. But overall, Joy Farm provided a much-needed respite for the increasingly successful poet.

The windows of Joy Farm provided a clear view of Mount Chocorua. The easternmost peak in the Sandwich Range of the White Mountains assuredly provided inspiration for Cummings. His days at Joy Farm were generally split into poetry in the mornings and painting in the afternoons. Chocorua's influence is particularly evident in his painting. Cummings called his visual art his "twin obsession." As he expressed it in a poem on the subject: "Why do you paint? For exactly the same reason I breathe."

Cummings's literary output was prolific, as he was the author of over two hundred poems, along with two novels plus plays and essays. Just a few of the honors bestowed on him for his work, much of it produced at Joy Farm, were the National Book Award for 1957, the Bollingen Prize for Poetry in 1958 and the Shelley Memorial Award for Poetry in 1945.

BEYOND THE PAGE

The Madison Historical Society holds many personal items of the Cummings family donated on the death of Cummings's wife, Marion Morehouse Cummings. Also at the historical society are two paintings by Cummings donated by the family of Jesse Shackford Jr. The Madison Historical Society is located at 19 East Madison Road. The Historical Society Museum is located at Madison Corner and is open from 2:00 to 4:00 p.m. each Tuesday from June through Labor Day and by appointment. Contact number: 603-367-4640.

The Joy Farm was designated a National Historic Landmark in 1971 but at present is a private residence.

Chapter 25

HANS AUGUSTO REY AND MARGARET REY

1898–1977 and 1906–1996
Waterville Valley

Did you ever notice how many of Curious George's adventures involve close calls and riding a bicycle? He comes by it naturally. Many of the authors in this book came to New Hampshire from away. But none followed a more dangerous or circuitous route to reach their destination than German authors and illustrators H.A. and Margaret Rey. Thankfully, the couple's escape from wartime Europe was successful. That allowed the world to eventually enjoy the exploits of Curious George, the world's most beloved monkey. As German-born Jews working in Paris, the Reys recognized they would have to leave as the Nazis approached the city. On bicycles (built by Hans) and trains, the Reys fled down the Iberian Peninsula, traversing Spain and then Portugal, where they were able, barely, to escape by boat to Brazil. From there, they sailed to New York to begin life in the United States, where they would reside for the remainder of their lives. A move to Cambridge, Massachusetts, and the building of a summer home in Waterville Valley would complete the trip.

Curious George is the most familiar of the characters associated with the Reys. He was created in their image. When they made their way to Waterville Valley in the 1950s, they brought with them their trademark curiosity and love of learning. That curiosity knew almost no bounds and is represented today through the work of the Rey Cultural Center.

Curious George, the Reys' now-famous tailless monkey, made his first appearance in a 1939 book titled *Cecily and the Nine Monkeys*, published in Paris. The book tells the story of George and a family of monkeys and their relationship with Cecily the giraffe. From there developed the famous monkey the world has come to love as a collaboration of Hans and his wife, Margaret. Published by Houghton Mifflin in 1941, the original story was titled just *Curious George* and follows the now-familiar story of George and his adventures with the Man in the Yellow Hat. That was just the beginning, of course, as the Reys went on to tell of how George, in subsequent tales, takes a job, rides a bike, gets a medal, learns the alphabet and goes to the hospital.

Perhaps the other title that most exemplified the Reys' love affair with learning was 1952's *The Stars: A New Way to See Them*. The love of astronomy and the night sky was a key part of the Reys' enjoyment of the Waterville Valley area.

BEYOND THE PAGE

The Rey Cultural Center is located at 13 Noon Peak Road in Waterville Valley. The center offers programs aimed at honoring the Reys' spirit of curiosity for young and old as expressed in the nonprofit's mission statement: "The Rey Cultural Center honors the Reys' spirit of curiosity and discovery by increasing understanding of and participation in the arts, sciences, nature and literacy through programs for youth, adults and families." Contact the Rey Cultural Center, 13 Noon Peak Road, PO Box 286, Waterville Valley, NH 03215. Telephone: 603-236-3308.

PART IV

—◆◇◆—

MORE PEOPLE TO KNOW
AND PLACES TO GO

Chapter 26

NATHANIEL HAWTHORNE

1804–1864

He never lived in New Hampshire and is more closely associated with tales of his native Massachusetts, but Nathaniel Hawthorne left his mark on the Granite State. His fascination with the North Country of New Hampshire resulted in three of his most famous stories. It was also on a visit to the north of New Hampshire that the famous author of *The Scarlet Letter* passed away.

"The Great Carbuncle" and "The Ambitious Guest" were both White Mountain–inspired stories appearing in 1835 in separate issues of *New England Magazine*. In the former, Hawthorne tells the tale of the search for a precious gem. Eight adventurers with differing motives seek the gem in a typical Hawthorne examination of good and evil, the perils of selfishness and the virtues of simplicity. In the latter, a fictionalized retelling of the story of the Wiley family tragedy is presented in similar style. The story of the rockslide that wiped out the entire family was well known in the area. Hawthorne's retelling built on the fascination with the fate of the nine who were buried while fleeing their home.

"The Great Stone Face" first appeared in the abolitionist newspaper the *National Era* and is probably the best known of the author's White Mountain stories. It is based on the visage of the famous Old Man of the Mountain and what different observers read into its appearance. The search for a man to match the mountain leads the narrator, Ernest, to experience the folly of physiognomy. In the end, Hawthorne extols the wisdom of inner seeking rather than dependence on popular whims. " The

Great Stone Face" further popularized the tourist appeal of the famous face on Cannon Mountain.

From the White Mountains to the White House, Hawthorne was also connected to the Granite State through his long friendship with Franklin Pierce. The two were classmates at Maine's Bowdoin College, and the ties they formed there remained strong until they were literally broken by death. Pierce, of course, was New Hampshire's only holder of the presidency. In one of his less artistic endeavors, Hawthorne even cranked out a campaign-style biography after his friend secured the Democratic nomination.

In 1852, Hawthorne visited the Isle of Shoals and described his visit in *American Notebooks*, published in 1868. He stayed at the Appledore Hotel. The hotel was run by Thomas Laighton, father of young Celia, who was to go on to literary fame as Celia Thaxter. Hawthorne's journal entries provide a contemporary look at the islands and their inhabitants.

In 1869, Hawthorne's health continued what had already been a precipitous decline. Pierce accompanied his old friend to the White Mountains for a holiday. The hope was that exposure to the healthy air of the North Country might rejuvenate Hawthorne both spiritually and physically. Alas, while the author's spirits were undoubtedly buoyed by the time in a favorite place with a favorite friend, physically, time had run out. The two travelers stopped by Plymouth's Pemigewasset House on their return. It was Hawthorne's final sleep, as he was found by Pierce to have passed in the night.

It was an ironic and perhaps fitting end, as it further sealed his connection to the state. Neither born nor reared here, Nathaniel Hawthorne became forever associated with New Hampshire through both his writings and his fate.

Chapter 27

WILLIAM DAVIS TICKNOR AND JAMES T. FIELDS

1810–1864 and 1817–1881
Lebanon and Portsmouth

William Davis Ticknor and James T. Fields were born and raised on opposite sides of the Granite State. They also brought opposite talents to their eventual partnership in Boston. But once they merged, the result was one of the most successful and legendary American publishing companies of all time.

William Davis Ticknor was born and educated in Lebanon, New Hampshire. He did possess a bit of literary pedigree, as writer George Ticknor was his cousin, but his interest seemed to tend toward the business end of things. At seventeen, he left New Hampshire for Boston, where he worked in his uncle's brokerage firm and, later, at a bank. In 1832, he joined forces with John Allen and established the publishing house of Allen and Ticknor. James T. Fields was born in Portsmouth in 1817. His stay in New Hampshire only lasted until he was fourteen, when he was also lured south to Boston, taking a job at the Old Corner Bookstore. When Ticknor and Fields joined forces in 1839, it was James T. Fields who brought the literary intuition to the firm. First, he was a writer himself, publishing popular poetry and essays. Perhaps more importantly, he was highly successful in recognizing both literary promise and talent in others.

So the stage was set when Ticknor and Fields Publishing officially came into being in 1845 as Fields moved from junior to full partner. With Ticknor at the helm on the business side of things and Fields directing the company's course on the literary side, the roster of authors under the company's imprint reads like a who's who of nineteenth-century literature. Among others, Henry Wordsworth Longfellow, Nathaniel Hawthorne, Mark Twain, Charles Dickens, Harriet Beecher Stowe and Henry David Thoreau were all published with Ticknor and Fields.

Operating out of the Old Corner Bookstore in Boston, Ticknor and Fields also became a gathering place for the literati of Boston and the United States. Its status earned the Boston store and publishing house the title of "the hub of the Hub." It was a time when books and authors were an integral part of life in New England and the United States—and two young men from the Granite State were key to that status.

Chapter 28

ROBERT WILLIAM MONTANA

1920–1974
Meredith

I f you grew up enjoying Archie Comics, you might want to stop by Community Park in Meredith and say hello to America's forever teenager. There you will find a statue of the always smiling comic redhead waiting to welcome all visitors.

Archie was created by Bob Montana in 1941 as a character for Pep Comics. The new creation's popularity was such that, since the first Archie Comic appeared in 1942, the series has been an American constant. Of course, the Archie statue's location is anything but random. Created in 2018 by sculptor Valery Mahuchy, the life-size bronze is also a tribute to creator Montana, who lived and worked in Meredith for thirty-five years.

Most of Robert William Montana's teenage years were spent at Haverhill High in Massachusetts, and many of his iconic creations were based on friends and acquaintances from those days. But Montana's final year of high school was at Manchester Central, from where he graduated in 1940. Following graduation, he spent three and a half years in the Army Signal Corps during World War II.

When Bob was growing up, he and his family spent several summers in the Lakes region of New Hampshire. Following the war and a short stay in Manhattan, Montana and his wife, Helen, decided that Meredith was the place they really would prefer to live and work and, most importantly, raise their family. So it was that in 1948, they purchased a farmhouse in Meredith. Montana continued working at the Archie comic strip and living and raising

Bronze Archie statue in Meredith. Dedicated in 2018, Archie sits across the street from the studio of his creator, Bob Montana. *Melissa Crooker photograph.*

his family for thirty-five years in the small-town environment he had enjoyed during his youthful summers. It was there that he succumbed to a heart attack while cross-country skiing in 1975.

Meredith was a key component in the life of one of America's most successful cartoonists. As a plaque dedicated to Archie and his park bench on which he sits explains, he was also a valued and much-loved member of the community:

> *Bob Montana, 1920–1975. The genius behind Archie and his gang, proud to call Meredith his true home for 35 years, Bob loved our town, often putting local people and places in his comic strip. He gave his time, energy and talent to organizations and causes that benefited New Hampshire lives. His humor, creativity and leadership made Meredith a better place.*

Chapter 29

HORACE GREELEY

1811–1872
Amherst

Horace Greeley is perhaps best remembered for popularizing the phrase "Go West, young man." The phrase may or may not have originated with Greeley, but he made his name in life by going not west but a little south, heading for New York City from his native Amherst, New Hampshire, when he was twenty years old. Despite the success he enjoyed in life as a newspaper publisher and sometime politician, it was the lack of success on the part of his parents that made his stay in New Hampshire a short one. When he was just nine, his family, quite unsuccessful farmers, fled to Vermont to avoid debts. It was there that Greeley was apprenticed out to a printer in Vermont, setting him on the career path that would make him famous.

After learning the newspaper trade, Greeley helped found a literary paper called the *New-Yorker* in 1834 and, later in the decade, became involved with politics. He issued several political campaign weeklies for the Whig cause during the 1838 and 1840 elections. He served out the term of David S. Jackson as representative of New York's Sixth District.

That was to be his last successful effort for political office, but big things were ahead in publishing. In 1848, Greeley established the *New York Tribune*. After a slow start and paltry circulation numbers, the paper reached a near two hundred thousand circulation in the 1850s. With Greeley as editor, the paper first supported Whig policies and then took up the causes of the newly formed Republican Party. His editorials and opinions were widely read but difficult to pigeonhole. At different times in his career, Horace Greeley was a fervent supporter of Abraham Lincoln but later failed to support him for reelection. He supported abolition of slavery but signed the bail bond for former Confederate president Jefferson Davis in 1867.

Greeley also contributed to the Civil War literature of the time with his two-volume *The American Conflict: A History of the Great Rebellion in the United States of America, 1860–1864.*

Politically, Greeley's last hurrah, almost literally, was his unsuccessful bid for the presidency in 1872. Running on the Liberal Republican ticket, Greeley was crushed by Grant in the Electoral College by a 286 to 66 margin. But the official tally was even less close, as Horace Greeley fell ill and died before the electors were able to meet and his votes were split among four other candidates.

BEYOND THE PAGE

Located at the intersection of State Route 101 and Horace Greeley Road in Amherst is New Hampshire Historical Marker No. 3, giving this brief summary of Horace Greeley and his connection to Amherst: "About five miles north of Amherst birthplace of Horace Greeley (1811–1872), founder of the New York Tribune, member of Congress, and candidate for President in 1872."

New Hampshire Historical Marker No. 3 tells of Horace Greeley's birthplace in Amherst and his political and journalistic careers. *Gary Crooker photograph.*

Chapter 30

THOMAS STARR KING

1824–1864

He never lived in New Hampshire, but T. Starr King wrote one of the more influential books about the state's White Mountain region. *The White Hills: Their Legends, Landscape, and Poetry* was published in 1859 and was one of the most read "back to nature" works of its time. Although he was a contemporary of both Ralph Waldo Emerson and Henry David Thoreau, King's work was more widely read in its day than either of the celebrated duo's.

Starr King Grange Halls in Jefferson and Gorham as well as a Jefferson Cemetery attest to the name recognition his tome won him in the Granite State. Mount Starr King in the White Mountains is also named for the Unitarian minister.

T. Starr King also played a key role in popularizing the idea of a more harmonious coexistence with nature on the West Coast. In California, he gained even more renown both as a nature writer and in political circles. California also made him the answer to a trivia question.

King moved to San Francisco in 1860 to serve the First Unitarian Church in that town. A stirring orator and staunch Union man, King earned the sobriquet "the orator who saved the nation." His efforts to keep California true to the Northern cause and his organization of the Pacific Branch of the United States Sanitary Commission made him a major influence in the way the Civil War played out in the West.

In addition to his patriotic speeches, Starr King also beat the drum for appreciation of the natural splendor in the West, much as he had done in

New England. Hence the trivia tie-in. Thomas Starr King helped popularize the White Hills in New Hampshire and had a peak named after him. In the West, the outcome was similar, as 9,096-foot Mount Starr King is located in Yosemite National Park. He is the only man to have a mountain named for him in both the White Mountain and Sierra Nevada ranges.

Chapter 31

CENTER FOR THE BOOK AT THE NEW HAMPSHIRE STATE LIBRARY

Concord

New Hampshire's Center for the Book was established in 2003. The stated goal of the center is "to celebrate and promote reading, books, literacy and the literary heritage of New Hampshire and to highlight the role that reading and libraries play in enriching the lives of the people of the Granite State." What's not to love here, fellow readers?

The center realizes these lofty goals through several programs.

A New Hampshire Authors' Room is located at the state library as part of its effort to recognize the Granite State's homegrown and related literary talent.

The International Dublin Literary Award is presented to a novel of high literary merit written in or translated into English and published within a specified period of time. The New Hampshire State Library is a nominating library.

There can be no greater cause in the promotion of books and literacy than the encouragement of excellence in books for beginning readers. Established in 2003, the Ladybug Picture Book Award is awarded to promote early literacy. Winners are chosen through a committee of children's librarians throughout the state. The award is now in its twentieth year, and the following books and authors have been recipients:

2003: Kate and Jim McMullan for *I Stink!*
2004: Keiko Kasza for *My Lucky Day*

2005: Judy Schachner for *Skippyjon Jones*

2006: Karen Beaumont and David Catrow for *I Ain't Gonna Paint No More!*

2007: Judy Sierra and illustrator Stephen Gammell for *The Secret Science Project That Almost Ate the School*

2008: Elise Broach and illustrator David Small for *When Dinosaurs Came with Everything*

2009: Leah Wilcox and illustrator Lydia Monks for *Waking Beauty*

2010: Florence Parry Heide and illustrator Lane Smith for *Princess Hyacinth (The Surprising Story of a Girl Who Floated)*

2011: Devin Scillian and illustrator Tim Bowers for *Memoirs of a Goldfish*

2012: Eric Litwin and illustrator James Dean for *Pete the Cat: I Love My White Shoes*

2013: Mônica Carnesi for *Little Dog Lost: The True Story of a Brave Dog Named Baltic*

2014: Chris Van Dusen for *If I Built a House*

2015: Drew Daywalt and illustrator Oliver Jeffers for *The Day the Crayons Quit*

2016: Jon Agee for *It's Only Stanley*

2017: Steve Breen for *Woodpecker Wants a Waffle*

2018: Jessie Sima for *Not Quite Narwhal*

2019: Troy Cummings for *Can I Be Your Dog?*

2020: Julia Sarcone-Roach for *There Are No Bears in This Bakery*

2021: Corey R. Tabor for *Snail Crossing*

2022: Meredith Crandall Brown for *Milk and Juice: A Recycling Romance*

For more information on the Ladybug Award and other Center for the Book activities, contact Mary Russell, director, 20 Park Street, Concord, NH 03301, 603-271-2866, mary.a.russell@dncr.nh.gov.

Chapter 32

NEW HAMPSHIRE
WRITERS PROJECT

Hooksett

T he fewer writers nurtured and encouraged, the fewer books will be
written. Without support and backing from groups such as the New
Hampshire Writers' Project (NHWP), there would be far fewer
writers. Established in 1988, the NHWP has supplied that backing for thirty-
five years.

Headquartered on the campus of Southern New Hampshire University at
2500 North River Road in Hooksett, NHWP offers opportunities, programs
and a sense of community to New Hampshire writers of all genres. Just a
few of the events and programs available to member through NHWP are:

Workshops on a variety of topics related to the craft of writing. Go to the
NHWP website for up-to-date details.

Three Minute Fiction Slams. In these events, hosted at selected locations
throughout the state, writers are invited to compete before judges and a
live audience. Original fiction pieces of no more than three minutes in
length are judged, and regional winners move on to the final statewide
competition for cash prizes.

Writers' Night Out. These events give those interested a chance to meet
regionally with fellow writers and discuss ongoing works and other author-
related subjects. The meetings are usually held on the first Monday of
each month at various locations. Check the NHWP website, https//
nhwritersproject.org, for locations.

NHWP also sponsors the Biennial New Hampshire Literary Awards. Winners are chosen in the categories of fiction, nonfiction, middle grade/young adult, children's picture books and poetry.

These are just a few of the projects of NHWP as it serves as a resource for the entire reading and writing community in the Granite State. To join or request information, email info@nhwritersproject.org or call 603-270-5466. Mail inquires may go to New Hampshire Writers' Project, 2500 North River Road, Manchester NH 03106.

Chapter 33

NORTHERN NEW HAMPSHIRE
BOOK SHOW

Concord

Nothing exemplifies the preservation of literary legacies more than regional antiquarian book fairs. In New Hampshire, that tradition is one of the oldest in the nation.

The Northern New England Book Show, held on the first Sunday in June each year, is the direct descendent of the New Hampshire Antiquarian Book Show, reaching back to 1974. That was the year the New Hampshire Antiquarian Booksellers Association first opened in Concord's New Hampshire Highway Hotel. When the iconic hotel was torn down in the late 1980s, the show jumped the river to its new home at the Everett Arena on Loudon Road. With just a couple of exceptions, the show has remained at the arena each year. Now entering its second half-century, the show continues

Browsers and buyers at the Northern New England Book Show, one of the oldest antiquarian shows in the United States. *Richard Mori photograph.*

to draw dealers from all the New England states. In addition, booths are manned by dealers from a dozen other states and foreign countries. Books and ephemera from all the authors mentioned in this book along with hundreds of others are on sale.

Now directed by Mori Books of Franklin, New Hampshire, the show takes place on the first Sunday in June each year. Fifty to sixty dealers in old and significant books and ephemera will be on hand to offer their wares. It's one more way to meet many of the authors not just from New Hampshire's but the world's past and present; it would be an excellent way to spend the day.

Chapter 34

EXETER LITERARY FESTIVAL

Exeter

Exeter, New Hampshire, is rich in the type of literary traditions explored in these pages. And in Exeter, those traditions are celebrated on the first weekend of April each year.

Initiated in 2018 by a group of interested and motivated citizens, the Exeter LitFest has become a vibrant part of a vibrant community. As in so many cases, the group's own mission statement best explains what it has created and hopes to accomplish: "To leverage our wealth of local literary treasure, in an environmentally sustainable way, to connect both residents and tourists to the diverse literary voices and places of Exeter, NH for the benefit of children and adults, the local arts community and local businesses."

The young LitFest has done just that in just a few short years. The weekend festival offers speakers and programs at venues including the Exeter Library and the Town Hall. Local restaurants and businesses get in on the celebration with literary-themed events and menus. Also offered are downloadable literary walking tours of Exeter.

In 2022, Exeter LitFest featured novelists Brendan Dubois and J.D. Barker. The two hundredth anniversary of the birth of local poet and political activist James Monroe Whitefield was celebrated. Local poets and authors also took part in the successful weekend.

To stay up to date with the next LitFest, go to the website at www. exeterlitfest.com and sign up for the mailing list. It will be a very literary way to kick off the vacation season.

Chapter 35

SAINT-GAUDENS NATIONAL HISTORICAL PARK

Cornish

Today, Saint-Gaudens is one of only two National Historical Parks in New Hampshire. The home of one of America's greatest sculptors is important to New Hampshire's literary legacy because it also served as the birthplace and centerpiece of the Cornish Art Colony. Literary lights considered part of the colony include novelist Winston Churchill, Frederick Remington, Percy MacKaye, Everett Shinn and Witter Bynner.

BEYOND THE PAGE

Saint-Gaudens National Historical Park is located at 139 St. Gaudens Road in Cornish, New Hampshire. Augustus Saint-Gaudens lived and worked on the grounds of his beautiful estate from 1885 until his death in 1907. Saint-Gaudens was one of America's preeminent sculptors, and his home was also the site of the origin of what came to be called the Cornish Art Colony. While many of the great sculptor's works are on display, much information is also available about the colony. The Visitor Center, Little Studio and New Gallery-Atrium Complex are open from 9:00 a.m. to 4:30 p.m. from Memorial Day weekend to October 31. The trails and grounds are open year-round during daylight for hiking.

New Hampshire Historical Marker No. 134, located on NH 12A, gives a short history of the Cornish Art Colony, which was a gathering place for artists and writers. *Melissa Crooker photograph.*

New Hampshire Historical Marker No. 134 is on Wilson Road in Cornish and commemorates the Cornish Colony:

The Cornish Colony (1885–1935) was a group of artists, sculptors, writers, poets and musicians who joined the sculptor Augustus Saint-Gaudens in Cornish and found the area a delightful place to live and work. Some prominent members were sculptor Herbert Adams, poet Percy MacKaye, architect Charles A. Platt and artist Kenyon Cox, Stephen Parrish and his son Maxfield, and landscape architects Rose Nichols and Ellen Shipman.

ABOUT THE AUTHOR

Gary Crooker has worked as a journalist and author for fifty years in his native New Hampshire. He has been a staff member of the *Milford Cabinet* (Milford, New Hampshire) and *Monadnock Ledger* (Peterborough, New Hampshire) newspapers. In 1994, he won Best Sports Story from the New Hampshire Press Association. He has worked as a columnist for the antique magazine *Unravel the Gavel* and for the children's magazine *Faces*. In addition, he has also worked as a truck driver, salesman, warehouse manager, high school athletic director and coach and bartender. Crooker has been a member of the New Hampshire Antiquarian Booksellers Association (NHABA) for over thirty years. He served as vice president of that organization for six years and as fair director for nine years.

A resident of Wilton, he has served on that town's school board and zoning board and as town treasurer and has been involved with the community's Old Home Celebrations for forty-five years. He is the author of *New Hampshire Old Home Celebrations* (Arcadia Publishing, 2009).